EMPLOYMENT

IN THE AGE OF

DRASTIC CHANGE

The Future With Robots

D.A. BELL   *F.I.E.E., F.Inst.P.*

Professor Emeritus of Electronic Engineering
University of Hull

ABACUS
PRESS

First published in 1984 by

ABACUS PRESS

Abacus House, Speldhurst Road, Tunbridge Wells, Kent, TN4 0HU

© Abacus Press 1984

Printed and bound in Great Britain by Woolnough Bookbinding, Wellingborough, Northants.

 British Library Cataloguing in Publication Data

Bell, David A.
  Employment in the age of drastic change.
  1. Labor supply——Effect of technological
  innovations on
  I. Title
  331.12'5   HD6331

  ISBN 0-85626-426-1

Professor D. A. Bell

(photo courtesy of University of Hull Photographic Services)

FOREWORD

The most pressing problem confronting the whole world and more immediately the western world is that of adapting our society to changing needs, these changing needs being primarily concerned with the fast developing worlds of science and technology. It has been estimated by a number of scientists that our factual knowledge (they are more guarded about the philosophical and metaphysical) has increased astronomically in the last 25 years; it has even been suggested that we have learned more (of the factual) in the last 25 years than in the whole previous history of man. The point, regardless of estimates, is clear and is that we are having the face of society dramatically changed. The whole world is in a state of flux.

In the present circumstances many, even most, people — especially politicians — talk in terms of the existing 'social democratic capitalisation' of the west, and seek to find ways of increasing competitive production and finding ever increasing markets and to eliminate unemployment as a result. To be competitive though they need to automate and automation, in a sense that is updated almost annually, inevitably decreases available jobs in the existing socio-economic framework. We must, at the macro level of political decision making, choose between two alternatives. One is seeking to find a whole range of new activities, much of which is what Professor Bell calls of 'communal benefit', but some of which can be the result of scientific and technological advances. The second alternative would be to restructure society in such a way that it would evolve into new social patterns, in which to work for a living would be no longer assumed. Rather it would be assumed that members of the community would all be provided with a sufficient income for mere existence, without any of the pejorative implications of unemployment and dole being attached to them. It could, of course, be that some compromise between (or conjunction of) these two approaches could be made.

The difficulties confronting us are how to ensure widespread prosperity in order to finance what I would prefer, for psychological reasons, not to call a 'welfare state' yet which in a sense is, and to avoid any suggestion of becoming any sort of communist community with any of the wholly unacceptable associations with the Soviet Union. That it can, nay must, be done is certain, because the easy arguments of those who say that the new technology will demand an ever increasing manufacturing population are surely wrong. The machine to make the machine and the machine to make itself are all on the drawing board and human labour becomes an inefficient luxury, and work will become a privilege.

Professor Bell has taken up the cudgel of arguing through the details of what might be attempted and what achieved. His arguments are well laid out and convincing, and he puts his finger on the bulk of the micro-ingredients of the macro argument. Nothing impinges more firmly on the problems confronting us than that which he calls 'education for life' in both the senses of this intentionally ambiguous phrase. It seems certain that if we are to survive and retain what is worthwhile in present society and yet also benefit from a scientific age of knowledge and plenty, then the key must be above all else in education in its very widest sense. This is itself a matter which requires detailed thought and analysis and like all change, must be introduced in an evolutionary manner, rather than by a sudden discontinuity in social progress.

To succeed in any of these vital quests, requires a detailed understanding of the problem and that is something which Professor Bell has and which his book well shows. It would be nice to think that our political and economic leaders had the same insight and could raise their gaze beyond the immediate struggle for survival to have some vision as to where we are trying to arrive; such vision is essential even to our immediate problems and absolutely vital to our future progress.

F.H. GEORGE.

PREFACE

The economic prosperity of the nation depends on a number of factors such as the condition of world trade, world and domestic fiscal policies, domestic politics, and also the efficiency of industry. The present work is concerned solely with one aspect of the organisation of industrial society, namely the effect of 'new technology' on the numbers of employees and skills required in manufacturing industries and the consequent reaction on service industries. This factor is believed to be dominant in the matter of unemployment, which is analysed on the assumption that other factors remain 'average'— e.g. it is suggested that a revival in world trade together with a successful outcome of domestic fiscal policies ('end of the recession') may absorb one million out of the present three million unemployed but would not provide full employment either then or in the long term.

It is often said that there is plenty of additional work waiting to be done, but on closer examination this is usually found to be work of *communal* benefit (maintaining or restoring sewers, roads and housing or clearing derelict inner–city land) which would have to be paid for by higher taxation in one form or another. It may be that in addition to a change of spending habits, the large–scale transfer of labour from manufacture to services will eventually require this higher taxation (unless the yield of existing taxes is sufficiently raised by higher industrial productivity) but any such change is closely linked with political attitudes. For the present, therefore, the part played by 'public works' is taken to be one of the 'average' factors and it is the future of commercial employment which is here explored.

The author wishes to acknowledge the stimulus and benefit gained from correspondence with a number of people during the writing of this book; and he wishes to thank a former colleague at the University of Hull, Professor A.D.B Clarke, for most helpful discussions and advice on parts of Chapter 5. The final conclusions on controversial points are, however, the author's sole responsibility. Much of the material in Chapter 4 appeared first in two Occasional Papers prepared for the Economic Research Council.

D.A.Bell
Walkington 1983

EMPLOYMENT IN THE AGE OF DRASTIC CHANGE:
The Future with Robots

CONTENTS

SUMMARY

The theme of this book is the need for change — change in the ratio of employment in production to employment in service industries, change of emphasis between employment and self-directed activities (leisure occupations) together with changes in organisation and in education which must underlie these material changes. Technology is now able to revolutionise production industry (and some parts of service industry) though it may take a considerable time to penetrate the whole of industry. Technology is the only factor which has been considered in this book. There is also a demographic factor, the number of people of working age; but this is complicated by the participation rate, i.e. the proportion of those people of working age who seek organised employment. Admittedly the demographic factor is more significant than usual at present, because the number of school leavers exceeds the number of those retiring. Expedients such as the extension of vocational training, work experience and job-splitting schemes can fairly be aimed at this temporary problem. This twin factor which controls the size of the work-force has been left aside; it may modify the numbers immediately involved, but it cannot change principles.

Chapter 1 reviews briefly the international scope of the problem. Chapter 2 reviews the ways in which Britain is disadvantaged in the industrial world. Of course the supporters of the 'green' or 'ecology' movement will say that they want Britain to be different, to aim at a peaceful pastoral life rather than the rat-race of industry, but the author judges that the majority of the British people are too attached to their 'mechanical toys' (cars, TV, home computers) and style of life (holidays abroad) to accept the pastoral ideal. Chapter 3 records the growth of technology while Chapters 4 and 5 examine its economic and employment consequences. Chapters 6 and 7 consider what organisational changes will be needed. Transfer from production to service industries and reduction in working hours are comparatively easy, if only because they are quantifiable and the continuation of historical trends. The serious problem is the future of the unskilled: if they will no longer be useful in industry, can they be eliminated from the population by education? There is disagreement among psychologists over the relative importance of heredity and environment in the distribution of intelligence and ideas on education are usually not based on quantifiable facts. Chapter 8 is therefore more speculative, though relevant facts have been mentioned wherever possible.

Chapter 1

AN INTERNATIONAL PROBLEM

Introduction

There seems little doubt that the 'world recession'of the 1980's was triggered by a steep rise in nominal oil prices from about $13.50 per barrel in January 1979 to $35.50 in January 1981, in current US dollars. These are described as 'nominal' prices, not so much to exclude the spot market, which handles only a very small proportion of the total quantity of oil, but because prices expressed in current dollars make no allowance for inflation. The oil producers claimed that the increase from about $11.50 in 1975 to $13.50 in January 1979 was not enough to cover the decline in value of the dollar. According to OECD (Organisation for Economic Co-operation and Development) figures[2] the implicit price level associated with the US dollar value of the GDP of USA rose by 55.4% between 1975 and 1981. This factor would have lifted the $11.50 price of 1975 only to about $18, roughly half the actual price. The very steep increase in price through 1979—1980 to the peak of $35.50 in January 1981 must have been based on the producers' idea of 'what the market would bear' and unfortunately this idea was wrong. There was a general decrease in economic activity, with consequent decline in the demand for oil; and in June 1983 the price had fallen to an average of $28.59.[1]

However, the price of oil is not the sole or long-term cause of *unemployment*, which depends also on changes in the methods for supplying the demand for goods and services. This problem of unemployment associated with industrial change affects many countries, but not all of them equally. For the purposes of this study the 'world' can be divided into several groups of countries. One first excludes those which in economic studies are given the non-political title of 'centrally planned economies', i.e. the USSR with its

East European associates and China, since unemployment is here theoretically non-existent. Then the 'third world' (much of Africa, India and some parts of Asia) is irrelevant because industry has so little effect on social organisation in regions where the main problem is still that of obtaining sufficient food. Even in this, however, their relationship with industrialised nations is relevant because the low prices which depressed economies will pay for commodities and raw materials, hinder the third world countries from importing food to meet emergencies such as drought. Besides the 'old' industrial countries of Western Europe and North America ('the West'), there remain the rising industrial countries and centres of Japan, Mexico, Korea, Taiwan, Hong Kong and Singapore; the developing countries of South America; and the oil countries of the Middle East.

Most of the oil-producing countries of the Middle East have ample oil revenue to pay for imports of manufactured goods and are little concerned with internal industry. Industrial development in Iran was rapid before the revolution, but its present status and future prospects are unknown and unpredictable. By analogy with the French Revolution, one might hope for the restoration of stability within less than a century.

When one turns to the major industrial nations, the first thing to note is that conditions now are not as severe as in 1930 — and we do not want them to be! Unemployment in the USA was 25% in 1933 and in spite of the New Deal there was only one year (1937) before 1941 in which unemployment fell as low as 14%.[6] (1941 was the year in which the Japanese attack on the US Pacific Fleet in Pearl Harbor brought the USA fully into the Second World War and put its economy on a war footing.) 'Soup kitchens' were widespread because there was little systematic provision of the type of welfare service which we now call 'social security' in Britain. Unemployment in the United Kingdom was 22.1% in 1932 and fell as far as 10.8% for only one year (1937) before the Second World War. The 'hunger march' from Jarrow to London was a spontaneous expression of the desperation of the unemployed which arose at that time, and had no external support other than the extempore provision of food and lodging by well-wishers en route. In Germany, one of the slogans used by Hitler in his successful 1932 election campaign was 'Brot und Arbeit' (bread and work). The climate of opinion has changed since then: it is now widely believed that 'the state' or 'the government' has an obligation to provide everyone with an acceptable minimum livelihood, traditionally through 'full employment' in the first instance. Governments usually refrain from defining an official poverty level because public expectations of the minimum level of livelihood rise over the years. The level of social security expected is now much higher than in the 1930's.

Populations have been steadily increasing, and in developed countries the participation rate (percentage of the population seeking paid employment) has also tended to increase, so that it is often true that there are now more people *employed* than a decade ago. On the principle symbolised by the saying that 'every child is born with a mouth as well as a pair of hands' one might expect employment to rise with population. None the less the percentage of unemployed is increasing, as well as the number. There are two other demographic problems. The first is that in Europe there are at present more people reaching the age to enter industry than there are reaching the age of retirement. This is a temporary phenomenon which does not affect the underlying trend and principle but exacerbates the immediate problem. The second is that increasing longevity increases the ratio of pensioners to workers and this is a lasting problem.

USA

In the early 1980's the USA suffered a sharp increase in unemployment and it has been suggested that the counter–inflation policy is similar to that in Britain — that 'Reaganomics' is similar to 'Thatcherism' and that both, while reducing inflation, have failed to eliminate unemployment. This may be so, but there are differences in the magnitude of the problems involved. The year–on–year inflation in the USA began to rise in 1979, reached 13.5% in 1980, declined to 6% in 1982 and 3.9% for April 1982 to April 1983, all in terms of the consumer price index for urban wage earners and clerical workers. In the UK the retail price index rose by 18% from 1979 to 1980 and its annual increase fell below 4% in July 1983.

On unemployment there is the factor of rising population and in fact in the USA *total employment* (in numbers rather than percentage of population) has increased by a factor of 1.29 times in the decade 1971—1981 and even employment in manufacturing industry increased 1.09 times. The ratio of 'goods related' to 'service related' employment has moved slowly down from 37.7:62.3 in 1960, to 31.9:68.1 in 1971 and to 28.0:72.0 in 1981. Nominal unemployment has always been higher in the USA than in some other countries: it was generally in the range 3.5% to 5.5% from 1950 to 1966 when that in the UK was 1% to 2%. It is possible that much of this is transitional unemployment (people changing jobs) so that the higher figure in the USA would be due to a greater mobility of labour. Unemployment in the USA rose to higher levels after 1973, probably due to oil price increase, whereas in the UK and several other European countries it began to rise in 1966. But in the USA there was some increase before 1974, since it averaged 5.4% over 1970—1973 compared with 3.7% over 1966—1969 (Annual figures are given in Table 1.)

The customary view in Britain has been that the USA lags in the provision of social security or 'welfare' (and in the growth of trade union membership) but leads in technology and standard of living. The difference in 'welfare' provision may be partly a matter of policy: most social security benefits in the UK are paid in cash which the recipient may spend wisely or foolishly according to his/her ability and inclination. This has led to complaints that benefits are abused by a very small number of the recipients. But in the USA, food stamps (i.e. vouchers which can be used only for the purchase of food) are an important factor; and in 1980 they were issued to 8.2% of all households. In the UK, on the other hand, the only departure from cash payments has been in relation to 'overhead' costs, e.g. the payment of rent directly by the Department of Health and Social Security. The difference between US use of material support and UK dependence on widespread cash hand-outs was even more pronounced in the past. At one stage of the New Deal the WPA (Works Progress Administration) in the USA was providing work of the most varied kind, from building local airfields to compiling specialised mathematical tables, while the UK unemployed received their dole in cash. Looking back from the 1970's to 1929—1939, a British author wrote:

> 'There is some significance in the fact that, while the British Government provided dole, the American Government supplied jobs. The old belief in salvation through hard work remained powerful, and salutary. The provision of work

Year	Unemployment %	Year	Unemployment %
1947	3.9	1972	5.6
1950	5.3	1973	4.9
1955	4.4	1974	5.6
1960	5.5	1975	8.5
1965	4.5	1976	7.7
1966	3.8	1977	7.1
1967	3.8	1978	6.1
1968	3.6	1979	5.8
1969	3.5	1980	7.1
1970	4.9	1981	7.6
1971	5.9	1982	9.5

Unemployment in the USA since World War II

Table 1

greatly helped the process of vindicating America's self–respect. Despite the greater severity of the depression in America than in Britain, the scars healed more quickly over there, and post–war and present–day economic problems have been and are easier to handle because of the much less acrid legacy of hatred from those years.'
(see Reference 6, p.155)

The shock is to find that the USA is no longer the unchallenged leader of the world in wealth production as measured by GDP per capita. According to EEC statistics for 1978, in EEC currency units, the USA had been surpassed by West Germany, equalled by Luxembourg and could well be challenged by the rapid rise of Japan. In 1981, however, the GDP of Japan was 252×120^{12} yen and the USA 2,888 x 10^9 dollars. With populations of 117.65 million and 229.8 million respectively and the nominal exchange rate of 220 yen to the dollar, this results in dollar figures of GDP per capita of 9,729 for Japan and 12,567 for the USA. The corresponding figure for Germany is 11,077 dollars, so that America is once more leading, though by a fairly modest margin.

In the meantime the level of education in the USA is rising and Professor Peter Drucker has said[7] that 'American economic potential and production can no longer be based on native Americans doing manual labour. It must be based to the fullest extent possible on knowledge workers.' Alongside this statement he reproduces a labour force projection[8] that from 1978 to 2010 the demand for elementary–educated factory workers will increase while the supply decreases. The increasing demand is contrary to the argument of this book, but the supply projection presumably reflects US social trend and policy. What must be questioned is whether all those with more than elementary education will qualify as knowledge workers (see Chapters 6 and 8). Drucker also raises a delicate political problem in assuming that the residue of manual labour can be performed by residents in the USA who are not 'native Americans', whatever that may mean.

A reason why the USA should be able to survive the recession better than most European countries is its small dependence on overseas trade. On the other hand, it has never made use of 'guest workers' from poor countries. In the last resort these 'guest workers' can be eliminated from the labour force by sending them home, as has been done to some extent in Switzerland. No such option is available to the USA

It will be suggested in Chapter 5 that about 7½ million jobs in the UK are becoming obsolete. The labour force of the USA is about four times the size of that of the UK, so it is a remarkable coincidence that it has been suggested that steps must be taken to re-train 30 million American workers. A complement to the reduced employment in manufacturing industry (due to increased productivity) must be a continuing transfer of labour to service industries, probably faster than in the past, and there must also be the change from manual workers (including the skilled) to 'knowledge workers'.

Japan

Japan is already nearing parity with the West. Hitherto it has been expanding its industries rapidly and has had rather lower wage rates than the West and this is reflected in a lower value of GDP per capita. These two factors have enabled it to keep unemployment down to a level which compares favourably with that of other countries. There are also the factors that large firms give 'life-time' employment and that this life-time employment ends with retirement at the early age of 55. Some credit must also be given to the quality of Japanese management, the climate of industrial relations and the recognition by Japanese industry of the value of education. A period of rapid expansion also means that industrial plant can be up-to-date, without the problem of scrapping obsolescent but still serviceable plant (and workers). It may be said therefore, that hitherto Japan has been able to export its unemployment to the embarrassment of Western automobile and consumer electronics industries, and the anxiety of Western computer and microelectronics industries. For it must be recognised that Japan is no longer merely a low-cost producer and imitator of the products of other countries. It certainly leads in cameras and probably in video recorders. It is challenging for leadership in computers, with its 'fifth generation' concept, the establishment of a national committee (JIPDEC) to guide development and an invitation for international participation. With the approach of the end of the era of development, there is beginning to be anxiety in Japan about future employment. Over the decade 1972 to 1982 the official number of unemployed has increased from 730,000 to 1,360,000 representing a rise from 1.4% to 2.4% of the total work–force[2]. Before 1966, while unemployment in the UK was usually between 1% and 2%, a level of 2.4% might have been seen as an alarm signal; but there has since been a steady increase elsewhere, with figures up to 10—13%, so that anything below 5% appears creditable. Moreover it has been suggested[9] that the Japanese figures are unrealistic, for example because Japanese workers may move from being employed to being out of the labour force without passing through the state of unemployment. It is suggested that if the unemployment figures in Japan were calculated on the same basis as in the USA they would be much larger, though still smaller than the US figures, as shown in Fig. 1.

Unit labour costs in Japan have increased by a factor of 1.8 times over the decade 1972—1982 while GNP increased only 1.55 times (at constant prices). These are indications that Japan is approaching 'maturity' and may expect soon to experience some of the problems of the West. But it still has the advantage of less weight of old industrial plant and of inappropriately trained workers, compared with countries which experienced the industrial revolution a century ago.

Germany

Germany, 'the land of the economic miracle', is now following the same general trend as other countries. Unemployment as a percentage of the civilian labour force increased from 0.9 in 1971 to 7.5 in 1982; and employment in *manufacturing* industry decreased by 18% over the same period[2], corresponding to the usual movement from production to service industries. Accompanying the increase in unemployment is the decrease in number of notified vacancies from 648,000 in 1971 to 104,000 in 1982. Over the period 1971—1981 the total number of insured workers decreased by 1,532,000 (6.9%), out of which the reduction in number of foreign workers was 198,000. Looked at another way, the peak year for total employment was 1973 and the peak year for foreign workers was 1974. Starting from the levels of these years, the decreases to 1981 were 8.2% in total and 21% for employment of foreign workers[10]. From 1976 to 1981 the foreign workers constituted between 9% and 10% of the total.** In

% Unemployment

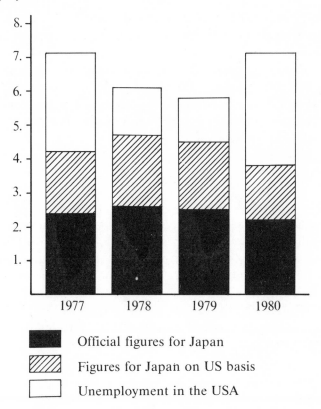

Figure 1

Unemployment in Japan:
official figures and estimates on US basis.

fact unemployment was spread fairly uniformly up to 1979, the percentage of foreigners among the unemployed being about the same as their proportion of the work-force, but by 1982 the ratio of foreign:German workers among the unemployed had risen to 14.4: 85.6.

Germany appears to have a rather higher than average proportion of its workers in industry. According to a European Common Market report[11], using the NACE classification in which production and distribution of gas, electricity and water are included in industry but transport and communication are not, while agriculture (as is usual) is excluded from both industry and services, the industry:services ratio in Germany fell gradually from 55.3:44.7 in 1970 to 48.4:51.6 in 1980.

France

In France the number of unemployed rose over 5 times from 1971 to 1981, while the population rose only 8.4%. The newly elected President Mitterand in 1981 proposed to combat an unemployment figure of 1.77 million by a progressive reduction of the weekly hours of work (see Chapter 7 on work sharing) but his plan was halted in 1982 by financial difficulties. The index of employment in manufacturing industry (taken to be 100 in 1970) fell from 100.6 in 1971 to 90.0 in 1981.

Switzerland

Switzerland is unusual in that it has the lowest unemployment *and* the longest working week[†] in Western Europe. It would be natural to speculate about the possible contribution to this state of affairs of the pact between major trade unions and employers for no strikes and no lock-outs: the Peace Agreement in the Swiss engineering and metal-working industries has held since it was concluded on 19th July 1937. The number of registered unemployed *decreased* from 62,000 in 1971 to 5,900 in 1981 out of three million wage earners, i.e. a fraction of 1% in 1981. It is reported to be 30,000 in 1983, still not more than 1%. It is true that Switzerland has had foreign workers as a 'buffer', but their proportion in the work-force does not appear to have varied drastically: it fell from a maximum of 26.1% in 1973 to 22.6% in 1981. The difference of 3.5% would be very significant on the Swiss scale of under 1% unemployment, but still would not bring Switzerland up to the level of other countries. The Swiss say that the decline in their watch industry (a fall in employment in the watch and jewellery industry of 25% between 1975 and 1982) was due to world over–production. But part of this extra production is represented by the introduction of very cheap digital electronic watches which do not need the refined mechanical workmanship of the traditional Swiss watch. Moreover in the quartz–analogue type of watch, which does include some mechanical parts and is roughly ten times as expensive as the simple digital watch, a Japanese make is prominent. In general pattern, however, Switzerland follows the world trend in that employment in industry (the'secondary sector' in Swiss terminology) decreased by 78,900 (6.3%) between 1975 and 1982 but employment in services (the 'tertiary sector') increased by 118,900 (7.8%) with the biggest single item being 34,300 in health services, followed by 19,800 in banking. Agriculture etc. (the 'primary sector')decreased by 23,800 (10%).

Mexico

Mexico is in an intermediate position as a rapidly industrialising country. According to an internal source[4] its industrial production contributes 25% of its GDP and 20% of its employment and ranks tenth largest in the non–socialist world, above the Netherlands and Belgium. The population of Mexico, however, is at least five times as great as that of the two countries mentioned. Unemployment in 1981 was 4.5% and the large overseas debt was attributed to high capital investment. But Mexico relies on commodities for its export trade and has been adversely affected by a fall in prices of coffee, raw cotton, blister (unrefined) copper, lead, silver* and *oil*.

Unlike most industrial countries, Mexico is a net exporter of oil on a considerable scale and therefore favours the high price of oil which is regarded by others as damaging to their economies. The basis of calculation of the 4.5% unemployment is not known but it is likely that a good proportion of the 80% *not* employed in industry are engaged in agriculture, some on a subsistence basis and some producing the cash crops of coffee and cotton. Its industry is probably too recent and expanding to suffer immediately from technological unemployment, though it may suffer from increasing market competition due to developments in other countries.

South America

The prominent countries in South America (Brazil, Argentina, Chile) are probably not yet fully dependent on industry, though industrial development is significant in Argentina and all of them think in terms of an industrial society. Their 'modern' outlook is most dramatically illustrated by the fact that at one time the President of Chile proposed to put the national economy on a computer.[††]   The proposal was to use the computer 'on line', not merely for modelling. It has also been reported[5] that Brazil has shown in exaggerated form the tendency that has been politically controversial in Britain, namely that 400,000 industrial jobs have been lost but 500,000 jobs gained in public service. But these countries also suffer variously from social unrest (as evidenced by the presence of militarily imposed governments) and dependence on foreign finance. In such societies, where there is little official welfare provision, it is difficult to tell how much unemployment there is and how much of the visible poverty is due to unemployment — in the Western sense of a malfunction of the industrial system — and how much to other factors such as the movement of population from an impoverished rural area to urban centres. North–east Brazil has recently suffered a drought lasting several years; but conditions have always been so harsh in that region that the population has tended to drift away to the towns unless active measures were taken to improve conditions, as described in a book published in 1972.[12]

East Asian Centres

Because the 'centres' in East Asia (Hong Kong, Taiwan, Singapore) were originally regions of low wages and hence low labour cost, they exported low-priced textiles and simple hardware; and it later became usual for Western firms to send electronic components there for any labour-intensive stages of manufacture: examples are the assembly of magnetic–core memories when they were used in computers and now the packaging of silicon chips. However it would be wrong to think of these centres as merely places where nimble–fingered girls assemble components for a bare subsistence wage. Expertise is also being gained, and some of these centres are under–cutting Western sources in the complete manufacture of electonic and other consumer products. Singapore is endeavouring to raise its level of expertise rapidly. It has appointed British personnel for the initial establishment of a course for the Higher National Diploma in Computer Studies (a two–year full–time course for high–grade technicians, a little below university degree standard and less academic) modelled on the UK polytechnic pattern. This is to produce 200 out of a total of 700 computer professionals; and there are also to be a few university graduates with two years of postgraduate work in Western institutions. Another indication of activity in Singapore is that a West German computer firm ran a two–day seminar there on Advanced Information Technology Opportunities, in June 1983. The political uncertainties about Hong Kong could help Singapore to gain a leading position.

Development has not yet gone so far as to nullify the traditional advantage of low–labour–cost regions and unemployment is not yet publicly visible. But wages are rising and when they have risen sufficiently the entrepreneurs will install more capital equipment — automation — so as to reduce labour requirements.

Summary

The examples from the Western world show the common trends to higher unemployment and movement from manufacturing industries to services; but detailed international comparisons are difficult because of differences in the methods of recording statistics. As an extreme example, a change in Denmark from measuring unemployment as the percentage of *insured workers* to measuring it as the percentage of the *whole civilian labour force* changed the figure by about 3:1. There is also difficulty about the estimation of number of vacancies, though they are obviously of crucial importance: long-term unemployment is to be expected only when the total number of vacancies is substantially less than the number of unemployed. In the UK the total number of vacancies is unknown but is reckoned to be about three times the number notified to the government 'Job centres'. In some countries there is no figure for *number* of vacancies but only an index (e.g. based on a value of 100 in 1970) of the amount of advertising described in USA as 'help wanted'. One would like to compare numbers employed with output in manufacturing industry; OECD statistics give employment in manufacturing industry but output under the broader heading of industry. These problems can be partly overcome by using the ratio of the values of the same quantity in 1971 and 1981. But there are still two defects: (a) one has no measure of productivity, owing to the lack of a figure for production from manufacturing industry and (b) the number employed will also be a function of the size of population, the participation rate (proportion of the population of working age in the labour force) and the working hours. The last point is considered in Chapter 7 on work sharing but there has been comparatively little change over 1971—1981. The following table of ratios of values 1981/1971 is therefore limited to (a) nominal unemployment, (b) a measure of vacancies, (c) unit labour cost and (d) consumer prices. It will be noted that there is a tendency for consumer prices to change in much the same way as unit labour cost (except in France).

In most industrialised countries unemployment has been drifting upward since 1966. (See Appendix, section 8.) A general survey by the OECD[3] now predicts a new peak in unemployment in 1983 of 9.5% over the whole of its 24 member countries, which represents 35 million persons. For Europe it forecasts 12% (20 million persons); and within this figure it forecasts for 1983 nearly 24% of youth (under the age of 24) unemployment in Britain and France and 41% in Spain. This is in spite of forecast growth rates of 1¾ to 3%. The problem of increasing unemployment affects immediately the countries with well-established industrialisation — broadly the members of OECD — but will affect other countries if they increase the sophistication of their economies on the same pattern. This widespread trend will not be halted until politicians realise that a reduction in *manufacturing* employment is inevitable and both politicians and public realise that this will require a change in education and in either or both of the method of distribution of personal incomes and the pattern of personal spending.

Country	Unemployment %	Vacancies	Unit Labour cost	Consumer prices
Canada	1.2	2.30	2.12	2.37
USA	1.3	1 .45	1.84	2.24
France	*5.3*	0.56	4.34	2.69
Germany	8.1	0.32	1.60	1.66
Italy	2.6	–	–	4.27
Netherlands	*6.2*	0.20	–	2.00
Switzerland	*0.1*	0.10	–	1.60
United Kingdom	3.0	0.54	3.70	3.70

– not available

figures in *italics* represent ratio of numbers unemployed, not %

Table 2.

Ratio of 1981 to 1971 values

NOTES

* At one time the United States used to maintain an artificially high price for silver, apparently largely for the benefit of Mexico.

** The number of foreign *residents* in West Germany is about twice the number of foreign *insured workers*: in round figures the numbers were 4½ million and 2 million in 1981.[10]

† Working hours are discussed in Chapter 7.

†† President Allende recruited a British expert, Stafford Beer, for this project, which was dropped on the overthrow of Allende.

References

1. *Petroleum Economist*. Published monthly.
2. *OECD Main Economic Indicators*. Published monthly.
3. *OECD Economic Outlook 33*. July 1983 (Reviewed in *The Times*, 13th July 1983, p.13 and p.26.).
4. Sixth State of the Nation Report by the President of Mexico. *Review of the Economic Situation of Mexico*, no. 681/682, vol. 58, pp.248–325. 1982.
5. Brazil Finally Agrees to Take IMF Medicine. *The Times*, 20th July 1983, p.18.
6. J. Potter, *The American Economy Between the World Wars*. London: Macmillan, 1974.
7. P. Drucker, The next American Work Force. *Economic Development Commentary*, October 1981, pp. 3–10. (The National Council for Economic Development, Washington DC).
8. R.L. Bolin and F. Pena, US Labor Projections, *Journal of the Flagstaff Institute*, January 1981. (Flagstaff, Arizona).
9. Kuji Taira, Japan's Low Unemployment: Economic Miracle or Statistical Artifact? *Monthly Labor Review*, July 1983. vol. 106, pp. 3–10.
10. *Statistiches Jahrbuch für die Bundes Republik Deutschland* Published annually.
11. *Employment and Unemployment Summary 1974–1980*. Published by the Statistical Office of the European Common Market.
12. P. Benton, *One Man Against the Drylands*. Collins and Harvill Press, London, 1972.

Chapter 2

IS BRITAIN DIFFERENT?

Why is the United Kingdom suffering more than most industrial countries in the world recession of the early 1980's? This is a politically controversial question and since the theme of this book is factual such political arguments are discussed in the Appendix. None the less there are some facts which can be examined.

The first fact is that Britain is no longer one of the most wealthy countries. Some years ago the author said to a young man 'Do you realise that Britain will soon be one of the poorest nations in Europe? Aren't you worried about it?' He replied 'No. Why should I be? Everyone is comfortable.' It is still true that most people (80—90% who are still in employment) are comfortable. In addition to general impressions, exemplified by a paragraph in the *Times* entitled 'Tills ring merrily' which referred to flourishing retail trade in Newcastle (an area of high unemployment), and by talk of the spending of redundancy money, the Monthly Digest of Statistics (Published by the Central Statistical Office) shows that the *volume* of retail sales has been increasing slowly while unemployment increased rapidly. But unemployment running at a national average of over 12%, and the suggestion that this was a major cause of riots in the poor quarters of cities (Brixton, Toxteth), ought to have shaken the belief that 'everyone is comfortable'. Table 3 shows a comparison of the UK with other countries in terms of both GDP per capita and unemployment. International comparisons of GDP per capita are difficult because of the need to use a common currency coupled with the fact that conversion by exchange rates does not always correspond to purchasing power. Therefore the figures in Table 3 have been taken from a report by the European Statistical Office (of the Common Market) for the year 1978. The vacancy ratio, the number of unemployed persons divided by the number of vacancies, was published by the OECD for the 4th quarter of 1980. The unemployment and vacancy figures must be

Country	GDP per capita 1978, in ECU†	Unemployment % Dec. 1980	Aug.1982	Vacancy ratio 4th.Q.1980
W. Germany	8190	4.6	6.8	3.5
France	6956	8.0	8.6	18.5
Italy	3604	7.1	10.4	–
Netherlands	7340	8.1	10.5	7.4
Belgium	7566	13.2	14.6	66.7
Luxembourg	7640	–	–	–
UK	4345	8.8	12.8	20.4
USA	7602	7.4	9.8	2.0
Japan	6720	2.2	–	–

† ECU is the common currency unit of the Common Market.

Table 3

treated with some reserve, since the method of counting varies in different countries; but they indicate the general trend. Of the countries listed, only France, Belgium and the UK had a vacancy ratio worse than ten to one in late 1980. Although unemployment is substantial in USA, the difference in 1980 was that the vacancy ratio there was only two, compared with twenty in the UK.

The first fact, then, is that Britain is no longer a rich country in terms of the usual measure of 'GDP per capita'. Sometimes GNP is used instead of GDP, but the two are near enough to be interchangeable in the first approximation. Gross domestic product may be regarded as being the value of all goods and services which are produced in the country, and gross national product as the sum of everything which can be bought in the country. GNP differs from GDP mainly through the subtraction of exports and the addition of imports; and exports and imports must roughly balance over a period of years.

The second fact, shown in graphs of competitiveness in OECD Main Economic Indicators, is that over the period 1979—81 unit labour costs in the UK rose 58% above the general trend, though by the first quarter of 1982 this figure had fallen to 35%. Since the UK has in general a low wage level (compared with West Germany or USA, for example) this high unit labour cost indicates low productivity. Studies by the National Institute for Economic and Social Research show that productivity in the UK is about half that in other industrialised countries. The reasons for low productivity are politically controversial and are therefore reviewed in the Appendix.

Of course there are factors in the UK situation which are the subject of 'political' controversy (not necessarily party political), such as the effectiveness of the education system, the change from the individualist attitude that, 'the world does not owe you a living' to the welfare-state attitude that 'the Government owes everyone a living', class war and the effectiveness of 'monetary' control of the economy, but these will not be discussed here. It might be argued that in limiting discussion to matters which can be ascertained factually, this book is looking at symptoms and ignoring causes; but there are two objectives which are to be sought through investigation of the facts. The first is to penetrate the complacency of those who believe that, 'everyone is comfortable', but this may already have been effected by unemployment. The second is to show that political ideas are not enough but that industrial society needs to be reorganised: unemployment will not go away as a result of putting the clock back or of abstract generalisations such as nationalising financial institutions, relying on private enterprise or leaving the Common Market. Neither the Conservative party at present in power in the UK nor the Labour Party/TUC at the other extreme has suggested that there is any need for a change in the basic organisation of employment, although in France, the socialist President Mitterand immediately after election took steps to reduce the standard working week (see Chapter 7). The seriousness of the situation may be brought home by noting that if we continued to be satisfied with the present level of production (the 'everyone is comfortable' attitude) *but* productivity (defined as output per worker) were doubled to match that of other industrial countries, then unemployment in industry in the UK would have to be about 50% (the same figure would not necessarily apply to service workers, so the overall unemployment might be only 20% to 30%). If productivity is not increased to match that of other countries, one will need for ever what is popularly called 'a siege economy' to keep the UK separate from the rest of the world. Whether one prefers an undemanding life within a siege economy to open competition in the world economy is a political question; but one can note that the outward indication of the world's largest siege economy is the Iron Curtain. However, Table 3 shows that unemployment is a widespread problem, and even retreat into a siege economy would not automatically cure it.

Why is unemployment in the UK worse than in other countries? Is it due to 'natural' factors of geography and population density, or is it due to failures of organisation? Political enthusiasts of various colours have various scapegoats for causes, but this book will try to concentrate on the facts as they exist. The UK is primarily an island, with a high density of population and limited resources in food and basic materials; is it therefore more dependent on foreign trade than other countries are? A measure of the degree of dependence on foreign trade is the value of imports as a percentage of gross domestic product (GDP). From Table 4 it can be seen that the UK is not wildly out of line with West Germany, France and Italy; is less dependent on foreign trade that the Netherlands, Belgium and Luxembourg; and more dependent than USA and Japan. The position of the UK is exceptional only in its low dependence on

Country	Imports as % of GDP, 1978	% of fuel imported, 1980
W. Germany	21	58
France	19	81
Italy	24	90
Netherlands	45	5
Belgium	53	89
Luxembourg	82	100
UK	27	6
USA	9	33
Japan	7	100

Table 4

imported fuel, due to North Sea oil (the similar position of the Netherlands is presumably due to North Sea gas).

The next question is the *kind* of import and Table 5 gives a comparison of UK, Euro 9 (the Common Market in 1978), USA and Japan. Euro 9 includes UK, so that its figure is distorted where the UK figure is exceptional; and this applies to the import of manufactures, for which the UK figure was exceptionally high. Italic figures in the table give the ratio of exports to imports for the relevant item: for example, UK exports nearly as much fuel as it imports, but Japan has no significant fuel exports. In the nineteenth century it was claimed that Britain was 'the workshop of the world', implying that we imported raw materials and exported manu-factured goods. It is now Japan which behaves in this way; and a major anxiety in Britain is that too high a proportion of imports consist of manufactured goods which could be made in Britain. Could be — so why are they not? This leads to arguments about protectionism, which are summarised in the Appendix. The second notable feature is that UK net expenditure on imported fuel is small — about 14% of total imports in 1980 compared with 29% for USA and 50% for Japan. It is a diminishing proportion and will remain so for the next decade or two as the production of North Sea oil approaches its peak. It should also be remembered that Table 5 records transactions in merchandise, and 'invisible exports' make a major contribution to the UK balance of trade — about 37% of the value of total imports in 1980.

The foreign trade position of the UK therefore seems to be advantageous in respect of fuel and raw materials, average for food, but unfavourable for manufactured goods. Having got our total wealth (GNP, approximately equal to GDP) do we spend it wisely? The most obvious factor in relation to productivity, and one which has received a good deal of publicity, is capital investment. But this is difficult to estimate because the easy statistic to obtain is the total expenditure on plant and buildings, which is known as 'gross capital formation', and this includes replacement of existing capital (depreciation). However, international financial statistics now include 'consumption of fixed capital' as part of the national income; and subtracting this figure from gross capital formation gives a possible figure for net capital investment. The result for various countries in 1978 is given in Tb.6, and though the exact figures may be unreliable, they do indicate that net capital formation in the UK

% of imports

Sector	UK		Euro 9		USA		Japan	
Food,beverages and tobacco	12.4	*0.53*	13	*0.49*	8.6	*1.39*	10.4	*0.11*
Basic materials	8.1	*0.53*	12	*0.18*	5.2	*1.95*	21.3	*0.21*
Fuels	13.8	*0.93*	26	*0.16*	29.1	*0.09*	49.8	*0*
Manufactures	62.6	*1.02*	46	*1.82*	28.5	*1.70*	17.9	*4.7*

Figures refer to: UK, 1980; Euro 9, 1978; USA, 1979; Japan,1980.
Figures in italics are the ratio of exports to imports.

Table 5.

was low. An illustration of this can be found in the accounts of many large companies. When a company proudly announces that its profit is x% greater than last year it is automatic to ask whether x% is greater than the rate of inflation. But if one looks further one finds that the declared profit is on *historic* cost accounting and the accompanying summary in *current* cost accounting usually shows a smaller profit. Now current cost accounting includes some esoteric corrections but the important point is that it calculates depreciation in terms of the *replacement* cost of an asset rather than the *historic* cost, i.e. the price when it was originally purchased. It is obvious that in a time of high inflation the historic cost method of accounting invites firms to under-state depreciation in the profit-and-loss account and so have an element of 'consumption of fixed capital' in their income. To this extent, high inflation will automatically tend to produce low capital investment in real terms.

The difference between gross and net capital formation is further complicated by the fact that owing to technological progress one does not always replace like with like in making good depreciation. For example, a word processor may be bought to replace one or more typewriters and its cost naturally goes into gross capital formation. If the typewriters had been replaced by new typewriters, there would have been no net investment; but if the word processor costs more, it is fair to regard the difference as investment from our point of view. The same argument applies if a manually-controlled machine tool is replaced by a tape-controlled or computer-controlled machine. So the absolute figures in Tb.6 have to be treated with some reserve, but international comparisons should not be completely invalidated, since similar difficulties apply in all countries.

The percentage of GDP going into new investment is not the whole story, even if one can determine it: for the same percentage a rich country will be investing more than a poor country in actual value. The performance of the UK as shown in Tb.6 is then doubly low: first in having a low value of GDP and then in having a low percentage devoted to net investment. The two factors are not necessarily independent: a poor person tends to spend most of his income and have little saving. This would account for both Italy and the UK having single-figure percentages. On the other hand, USA with one of the higher values of GDP appears to have the lowest *percentage* of new investment. This suggests complacency with the already high value of capital per employee in US industry. Is it a coincidence that USA has

Country	GDP, ECU per capita	New investment % of GDP	ECU per capita
W. Germany	8190	11.0	901
France	6956	11.6	807
Italy	3604	9.4	339
Netherlands	7340	13.1	968
Belgium	7506	12.7	961
Luxembourg	7640	15.3	1169
UK	4345	7.7	335
USA	7602	7.0	532
Japan	6720	16.2	951

Estimated net capital formation in 1978, based on Common Market (Eurostat) statistics.

Table 6

foreign exchange and unemployment problems in the early 1980's, just like UK? But comparison of the status of Belgium in Tables 3 and 6· show that investment is not in itself a guarantee against unemployment.

The discussion so far has been on what we do with our money, but what do we do with our work-force? The important distinction is between 'goods–related' and 'service–related' employment, but in compiling statistics the distinction does not always seem to be logical. The 'public utilities'; gas, water and electricity supply, together with transport and communications, are often put in the 'service' category, although gas, water and electrical energy are tangible products and the last can enter into foreign trade (even the UK has a cross–channel link with France and on the continent it is common for electrical energy to cross frontiers). Transport and communications use the same technology as manufacturing industry and are susceptible to the same employment trends. In the US statistics, agriculture is for some reason excluded from 'goods–related'activity. In these terms the ratio of goods:service employment in the USA has remained roughly constant at 30:70 since 1975. In the UK, and using census occupational data with the broader coverage of goods–related activities, the historical trend has been from a goods:service ratio of 70:30 in 1921 to 57:43 in 1931 and 40:60 in 1971 for England and Wales. Agriculture presents difficulty because both full–time and part–time employment vary seasonally and because there is an ill–defined number of working proprietors and their families. The size of agricultural holding gives some hint of the relative importance of working proprietors versus hired labour; and Table 7 shows that the agriculture of the UK is very different from that of West Germany, for example, and more like that of USA, except that the latter has some very large holdings

So is Britain different? In terms of objective statistics the answer must be yes, in the following respects:

1. It has the worst unemployed:vacancy ratio of any industrialised country, except Belgium. (Table 3)
2. In 1978 its GDP per capita was the lowest among industrialised countries, except Italy. (Table 3)
3. It is exceptionally fortunate in requiring little import of fuel, with a near balance between imports and exports of fuel. (Table 4)
4. Manufactured goods form an exceptionally high proportion of imports. (Table 5)

Size of holding	% of no. of holdings		
	UK	W.Germany	USA
1–5 ha (2½–12½ acres)	13.9	33.3	
Over 50 ha (over 125 acres)	31.3	3.5	
<10 acres			8.7
>180 acres			39.2
Commonest size	>50 ha	1–5 ha	50–179 acres
% of total employment	1.6	1.1	
	(3.0†)	(6.3†)	

† Estimate of percentage of occupied population, including self-employed and proprietors.
Figures for UK and for USA are for 1980, for W.Germany 1978.
USA has to be shown separately because they have altogether seven size classes, compared with the European five.

Table 7

5. Its unit labour cost is higher than that of competitors.
6. Its estimated new capital formation is an unusually low percentage of GDP and therefore very low in absolute value. (Tb.6.)
7. Its usual size of farm is much larger than that on the continent of Europe and more nearly comparable with that in USA (Table 7)

Item (7) is a major factor in the continuing discord between Britain and the other Common Market countries. It is an obvious question whether (4) and (5) are the causes of (1) and (2). If so, one has to look for the causes of (4) and (5); but this leads to political controversy. (See Appendix.)

Chapter 3

THE DEVELOPMENT OF AUTOMATION

The background and motivation of this book is the 1980's crisis of unemployment throughout the industrialised part of the world (the differences between Britain and other industrialised countries were examined in Chapter 2, and the non-industrialised countries, commonly known as 'the third world', more generally suffer a crisis of food shortage). One of the anxieties about the future of employment is that technological developments, especially automation, may reduce the requirement for human labour far below the level to which we have been accustomed for the past half century. So long as most men (and women) had to labour to the limit of their physical endurance in order to achieve a minimum livelihood, any displacement of human labour by either animals or machines was accepted as an unmixed blessing and the development of technology, broadly speaking, raised the average standard of living. This is not to deny that wealth was unequally distributed, whether as a result of military/political power, religious faith or business/political acumen. The pyramids and royal tombs of ancient Egypt, the Great Wall of China, the medieval cathedrals, and the chateaux and stately homes of Western Europe all show that a conspicuous part of the wealth of any era could readily go to projects other than raising the standard of living of the common man. None the less, the average standard of living has risen as a result of technological developments. Over the last two centuries the availability of textile materials and of piped water (the latter making possible the indoor WC to replace the outdoor privy), have changed from being luxuries of the rich to necessities, and now central heating, refrigerators, washing machines and colour televisions lie on the border between luxury and necessity. Division of *labour*, however, has been practised throughout history. For example, the blacksmith would devote the whole of his time to producing metal implements which others would use in agriculture. Even at this early stage there must have been some use of money as a means of exchange. Now, *employment* (with wages in money) is regarded as equivalent to *livelihood*. Some people propose that this connection should be broken in the 'post–industrial society' but there are possible psychological and sociological objections to such a view of the future of society. The psychological objection is that some pressure towards work is desirable, whether based on the negative idea that 'if a man will not work, neither shall he eat' or on the positive idea that 'fame is the spur'. The possible sociological objection is that to distribute the wealth produced by a small working minority amongst the whole community would involve intervention by the state on a scale hitherto unprecedented even in 'centrally planned economies' (a politically neutral description of those countries which in principle exclude private enterprise). Such concepts as 'taxation', for example, would lose validity. This book therefore assumes the continuation of an industrial society in which 'wages' are paid for 'work' (services as well as the manufacture of goods).

Historically the change which practically marks the transition from medieval to industrial society, and which might even be compared in importance with the change from nomadic life to settled agriculture at a much earlier stage, was the change from 'cottage industry' to the 'factory system'. This separated the functions of *production* and *marketing*, and by transforming the craftsman from an individual entrepreneur to a wage–rewarded worker ('wage slave') provided the basis of the modern concept of *employment*. (The medieval master-craftsman did share the work with a few journeymen and apprentices, but they would have some expectation of setting up on their own eventually.) It should be recognised that although the factory system was essential to mechanised production, the converse was not true. The earliest available reference is a poetic description of the factory of John Winchcombe in Newbury, Berkshire, at the beginning of the 16th century[1]. This is described as an assembly of 200 looms in a single hall, supported by 100 women carding and 200 maidens spinning. (There may have been some poetic licence taken on numbers since it has been estimated that three to five spinning wheels were needed to supply yarn for one loom.) Another example of wage employment not associated with mechanised production was Boulton's 'manufactory'. After the move from Snow Hill, Birmingham, to a permanent home in neighbouring Soho,* the manufactory employed 1,000 men, women and children under one roof to make all kinds of hardware articles (buttons, buckles etc.) which Boulton then sold. Thus the separation of production from marketing, which is fundamental to present ideas on industrial employment,** anteceded the mechanisation which stimulated the growth of the factory system. It was only in the second half of the eighteenth century, in the textile industry, that mechanisation began to produce a dramatic increase in productivity (output per person) and to make possible new products. Kay's invention of the flying shuttle had the immediate effect of speeding up weaving so that there was difficulty in the supply of enough yarn. It also made the weaving of wide cloth easier than it had been previously, when the shuttle had to be sent in from one side and retrieved from the other side at each throw of the weft.

Moreover, the flying shuttle opened the way to the fully automatic loom which could be driven by external power, initially water power, to be followed by steam and then electricity. The simplest form of loom produces only plain cloth. Production of patterned cloth requires the warp threads to be divided into several groups which can be lifted independently according to the requirement of the pattern at each pass of the shuttle. Originally the selection of groups to be lifted was made by an assistant to the weaver, but Jacquard devised an arrangement in which the selection depended on perforations in a card (patented in 1805). A card was needed for each pass of the shuttle, but the cards could be joined into an endless belt for a repeating pattern. Weaving was now completely mechanised, for patterned as well as plain cloth.

The increased productivity of weaving out-ran the capacity of the spinning wheel to produce yarn and so motivated the mechanisation of spinning which was the foundation of a large-scale cotton textile industry, (the same spinning process is now used for man-made fibres, which are initially produced as very fine filaments, chopped into lengths known as staple and then combined by spinning to make a much thicker thread).

Thus mechanisation of spinning and weaving made possible the textile industry, which was one of Britain's major employers of labour for more than a century. At the same time, the need for external power to drive spinning and weaving machinery required the concentration of production in multi-machine factories and enhanced the division of labour between production and marketing. Instead of the individual weaver taking his cloth to market or to a cloth hall, the entrepreneur (capitalist) who established a factory also took responsibility for the marketing of the product (and the supply of raw materials). There had for centuries been merchants who acted as intermediaries between the mainly craftsman producers and the eventual consumers, but it was mechanisation which made the factory system almost universal and with it the severance of direct connection between the productive worker and the selling of his products.

Thus, the effect of the industrial revolution in the textile industry was the transfer of production processes from hand work in cottage industries to power-driven machinery in factories. The machines were strictly repetitive in operation but had the advantage of working faster that the hand-operated devices which they replaced, though producing only to a standard design. The effect on employment was to create a large volume of semi-skilled employment but reduce the scope for the craftsman who took responsibility for the design, production and sale of an article. It was left for 'automation', sometimes called 'the second industrial revolution', to have the capability of eliminating both unskilled and semi-skilled work.

One tends to think that 'automation' has developed through the mechanical, electrical, and electronic engineering industries, with the archetype of automatic control being Watt's centrifugal (flying weights) governor for controlling the speed of rotary steam engines. This is still to be seen, for example, on fairground traction engines used to drive electrical generators. Watt's objective was to obviate the need for a human operator to work the valve gear at each stroke for fear that the engine would overrun if the valves were fully opened. Yet as outlined above, the first applications of mechanisation were in the textile *industry* but consisted of *mechanical devices*, e.g. the flying shuttle, multi-spindle spinning machines, and power-driven looms. These resulted in some replacement of human activity, but specifically in a reduction in the requirement for human muscle-power which was associated with minimal brain-power. In the case of the Jacquard loom, however, the assistant who was replaced had had to use a little thought in order to raise the different groups of warp threads in the correct sequence. The Jacquard cards therefore, may be regarded as a *store of information* (compare the role of the modern punched card) as well as a mechanical device and resulted in a reduction of the requirement for both brain and brawn. The weakness of all repetitive devices however is that they cannot allow for any abnormal condition — such as the breaking of a thread in a loom — and therefore they require close human supervision of the process or else inspection and possible rejection of the product. The logical descendants of this kind of repetitive machine are machine tools working on a repetitive cycle, such as automatic lathes for manufacturing screws and cyclically operating machine tools which have been widely used in the automobile industry. The particular form initially used for machining operations (e.g. on engine cylinder blocks) was known as a *transfer line* and consisted of a series of machine tools with automatic transfer of the work-piece from each to the next and often there was some simple check that previous operations had in fact been carried out. The ultimate form of this was a Russian plant for making car pistons, reported by Lilley in 1955[2], which consisted of one long transfer line from input of metal ingot, through casting and many stages of machining, to the packing of the finished product. Only 9 men were employed, so that each piston required less than four man-minutes of human labour. The use of cyclically operating machine tools is sometimes known as 'Detroit automation'.

The essential feature of Watt's centrifugal governor, on the other hand, is that it took account of local conditions by sensing the speed which might, for example, be affected by changes in load on the steam engine. To this extent it behaved in an 'intelligent' way, reacting to varying conditions as a human operator would (or at least should). Since it handled variable information (in contrast to the fixed information in Jacquard cards, for example) it was the archetype of the information-handling or *cybernetic* machine, of which the most acclaimed current examples are robots which use microprocessors to manipulate the information. The use of such devices constitutes true *automation* with a general reduction in the employment of human operatives and the ultimate aim of 'sweeping the last man out of the factory'. In 1982 there were advanced automated factories which needed only a few maintenance personnel, but as early as 1955 Lilley[2] commented:

> '...the automatic factory, in which all unskilled labour will have disappeared, is technically possible, economically sound, and humanly desirable'.

This 'human desirability' will be discussed in Chapter 6.

Apart from the economic aspect, there are two further, related, aspects of the development of *machines* which in the long run are important for their impact on human employment. The first is 'doing the impossible'. That is to say there are some jobs which can be done by a suitable machine but which could not be done by a craftsman using hand tools. An early example is that it is said that Boulton's success in manufacturing Watt's steam engines owed much to the fact that Wilkinson had developed (for the manufacture of cannon) a boring machine which would bore out a cylindrical shape more accurately than had previously been possible. Closely related is the second aspect, that machine tools are repositories of skill. In this sense Maudesley's compound slide rest for the lathe was the archetype of machine tools. The point of the compound slide rest was that it positioned the cutting tool mechanically instead of leaving it to the operator to guide the tool free-hand. This meant in particular that it was easier to obtain *reproducible* results which made possible the 'interchangeability' of parts which we now take for granted. Traditionally, an elementary test of craft skill has been the ability to file a straight edge accurately, but the relevance of this is less clear now that the straight edge will in practice be cut by a milling machine. For a long time it was still a skilled craft to obtain the optimum performance from a machine tool: one should make allowances for residual inaccuracies in the machine, such as back-lash in lead screws, wear of the cutting tool and yielding of the tool support under cutting pressure. One also had to choose cutting speed and depth to suit the material in hand and desired quality of finish, as well as ensuring a sufficient flow of cooling fluid. All these factors are taken into account in modern machine tools which are either numerically controlled (NC) or computer numerically controlled (CNC)[†] so that the skill involved is transferred from a craftsman working *at* the machine to a programmer and computer which produce the instructions for the numerical control. The detail draughtsman — whose job was solely to produce accurately dimensioned drawings from which the craftsman could make the various parts — is now obsolete. The designer draughtsman — whose job is to decide on the shape of parts and the material from which they are to be made, after the general arrangement in which the parts are to fit together has been determined — is still required. But with computer-aided design (CAD) he works with a visual display unit (VDU) driven by a computer, instead of with a drawing board. The computer will draw on the VDU any desired straight line, arc of a circle etc.; and when the designer is satisfied with a complete drawing, the computer will produce a 'hard copy', that is a drawing on paper. This process of CAD can eventually be coupled to computer–aided manufacture (CAM) so that the information in the CAD computer can be used directly for the control of NC machines instead of being taken out in the form of drawings and then programmed in again for the NC.

It is becoming apparent that in the progress of automation the emphasis is on *information*. Development of a theory of information in its engineering context[3] was instigated by Shannon's work[4] on the theory of communication (of information). He introduced the concept that 'information' (in a certain sense) was an objective and measurable entity, which was independent of the medium in which it happened to exist, whether printed page, computer store, sound wave or modulated electric current. Whatever the medium, the 'information' could be measured in a standard unit, usually the *bit* (which is an abbreviation of 'binary digit'). The further point of a relationship between 'information' and *entropy* has been the subject of controversy from time to time. Without going into detail however, it can be said that a move from order to disorder represents an increase of entropy and a loss of information, or conversely that a move from disorder to order requires expenditure of energy to reduce entropy and create information. In many mechanised production processes the parts produced by one machine are dropped randomly into a bin but have to be correctly oriented before feeding into another machine. The restoration of order represents a reduction in entropy which can only be achieved by the expenditure of energy. Larger parts may be oriented by the intervention of a human operator: the author has seen a man continuously engaged in picking piston rings out of a bin in order to place them in an orderly manner on a spindle. Such operations are sometimes defended on the ground that the human operator *inspects* the items at the same time. For small parts such as the products of an automatic lathe or small metal stampings, the commonest device is the vibratory bowl feeder. This employs a bowl with an internal spiral track leading from the bottom up to the top edge. The bowl is vibrated vertically with an acceleration rather greater than that of gravity and at the same time given a rotational oscillation. The result is that parts are thrown up and land back on the track a little higher than the point at which they left it. A system of 'gates' and 'trap–doors' near the top of the track ensures that any parts which are either of incorrect dimensions or incorrectly oriented are thrown off the track to return to the bottom of the bowl and only correct, and correctly oriented, parts emerge for further handling. The necessary *information* is built into the system of gates and trap–doors, and the *energy* is provided through the vibratory movement of the bowl.

The vibratory bowl feeder is applicable only to parts which are (a) small, (b) of suitable shape, particularly in relation to critical dimensions and (c) able to withstand the considerable amount of jostling which occurs while they are in the pile at the bottom of the bowl. The development of robust and compact solid-state 'television' cameras — which do not involve high voltage, an evacuated glass envelope or length for an electron scanning beam — has made possible the 'visual' inspection of items on a conveyor belt,[5] with directed action to re-orient (or, if necessary, reject) items which are not immediately acceptable. This method is most readily applicable to articles which can be checked in silhouette: otherwise one would need multiple cameras to give a 3-dimensional inspection. The 'visual' inspection has the advantage of being able to check for the correct presence of holes or cut-outs within the outline, which would be difficult with a vibratory bowl system. On the whole, the vibratory bowl system and the visual inspection seem complementary for different types of object.

It is perhaps natural that automation has proceeded fastest in the field of electronics and related industries, since electronic devices made an essential contribution to most types of automation. A small example of the effect on employment of progress in manufacturing methods come from the manufacture of electric lamps[6] and radio valves.[7] The development of this mechanised manufacture is apparent from a comparison of the photograph of an early apparatus for evacuating electric light bulbs in Fig. 2 with that of the machine for evacuating valves in Fig. 3. The glass–blowing skill required in the early manufacture was completely eliminated from the mechanised process — see details quoted in Chapter 5.

Up to 1945 the manufacture of domestic radio receivers had been labour-intensive. The first stage was the assembly of a number of components onto a metal tray or 'chassis', the second was the interconnection of these components by hand soldering wires to their terminals, and the third stage was the adjustment by hand of various inductors and capacitances so that turning was correct over the range shown on the dial. In some cases the number of turns on coils was adjusted by

Figure 2

(from Fig. 7 on p.7 of Philips Technical Review, 1963/4 vol. 25 no. 1.)

Figure 3

(from Fig. 87 on p.91 of book by J. Deketh, *Fundamentals of Radio Valve Techniques*, published by N. V. Philips 1949).

(Photos courtesy of Mullard Ltd.)

stripping off turns until the inductance value was correct, but more usually the inductance could be adjusted by a movable magnetic core.

Now the first rule of automation is to avoid anthropomorphism—only Heath Robinson would apprach automation of the automobile industry by designing a machine to automate coach–building, i.e. construction of the vehicle body by screwing panels to a wooden framework. Rather than make a machine to perform the same actions as the human operator it displaces, one should change the method of manufacture to suit automation. (But see below on 'robots'.) Sargrove followed this policy when he developed his Electronic Component Manufacturing Equipment which would make radio receivers by milling suitable patterns into metal–sprayed bakelite plates.[8] For example, by milling a groove in such a way as to leave a spiral of metal, he produced the winding of a coil; and by metallising both sides of an area milled down to a controlled thickness, he produced a capacitor. The interconnecting wiring was represented by narrow strips of metallising which were left when the surrounding area was milled away. The lack of success of this scheme was probably due to the very limited range of electrical values of the components which could be manufactured in this way.

The breakthrough came at about the same time, in the form of the printed circuit which eliminated the labour–intensive wiring–up operation. This innovation was facilitated by the reduction in size of components (miniaturisation) which had been accelerated by military requirements as well as by consideration of consumer convenience resulting from reduction in bulk and weight of apparatus. A sheet of insulating material is perforated to accept the wire terminations of (miniature) components and on one side has a sheet of copper foil bonded to it. Photo–etching removes the unwanted areas of copper to leave a pattern of interconnection between the wires coming through the holes, and the wires are soldered to the remaining copper by passing the whole assembly across the surface of a bath of molten solder. The largest remaining item of repetitive labour was in the insertion of components, or more exactly their wires, in the boards, so component–inserting machines were devised. In the simplest form, each head of the machine carried a supply of only one type of component, so the board had to be suitably located under successive heads so that the various components would be inserted in the correct positions. This brings us back to the point about orientation of component parts, because the component-inserting machine can only operate on components which are correctly oriented and placed. Therefore it is usual for the components — such as resistors which have the form of cylinders a few millimetres in diameter and a centimetre or so long — to be mounted on a paper belt which is known as a 'bandolier' by analogy with a belt of ammunition. So although the labour of inserting the components in the board has been eliminated, some additionnal effort is required to assemble the components into bandoliers. It is possible to work with only a single head for inserting the various components if the different components are arranged in correct sequence on a single bandolier. One also has to provide a two-dimensionally controlled movement of the board to the correct position for the insertion of each component, instead of a uniform single movement from station to station with the position of the insertion head pre-set at each station. Thus one has to weigh the cost of two forms of additional 'information' against the cost of additional insertion heads. The printed circuit technique was further stimulated by the introduction of transistors to replace valves; and the associated reduction in power consumption and therefore in the weight of the battery in portable equipment, stimulated further miniaturisation. The printed circuit technique has survived the integrated circuit revolution (see below) with the difference that instead of an array of discrete components being mounted on the board it may now carry an assemblage of complete integrated-circuit units and may then be called a 'mother board'. The technique has been elaborated, particularly for use in computers, first by the use of double-sided boards and then by the use of multi-layer boards (multiple layers of insulating board and connections, but components on one outer surface only). These make it possible for different connections to cross (geometrically) without making contact.

The introduction of the integrated circuit (IC) with subsequent development to large scale integration (LSI) and very large scale integration (VLSI) is a part of the solid-state revolution which is radically changing electronic equipment. The fact which made the IC possible is that the transistor is (almost always) made from silicon. It is also possible to make resistors in a silicon layer and connections are added by evaporating metal onto the surface, so that a complete electronic circuit can be manufactured in a silicon wafer. The other important point is that all the components can be very small — dimensions of components are measured in micrometres (thousandths of a millimetre) — so that one arrives at the now familiar silicon chip on which the circuit can only be seen through a microscope. Its special feature is high capital investment in the design and in manufacturing equipment but low cost per chip once the plant has been set up. With LSI (large scale integration) it is possible to produce the central processor of a computer on a single silicon chip and this is the microprocessor. The next step is VLSI, which is equivalent to producing a map of half Western Europe in street–plan detail in an area of a few millimetres square.

The microprocessor makes possible the cheap microcomputer which is valuable in introducing people to computing. The low cost also allows for distributed computing power: the use of a number of microcomputers for routine tasks in place of multiple access to a large central computer which requires an elaborate operating system to serve so many users. For example, stock control may be carried out by a microcomputer in the stores. More important than the micro-computer, however, is the use of 'dedicated' LSI chips, which may often be cheaply available microprocessor chips, even though one may not need the full facilities of the microprocessor. These uses range from the digital read–out from a micrometer a weighing machine which multiplies weight by price per unit of weight to give the price for the transaction, to teletext decoders and 'word processors' which are able to manipulate and store text. The micrometer represents an elimination of manual skill, since the accuracy of a micrometer reading depends in part on the pressure exerted on the object to be measured[††] and in the digital micrometer this pressure is provided by an internal spring. Both the weighing machine which multiplies and the word processor, besides pocket calculators and electronic cash registers, minimise the exercise of elementary mental skills. We have thus passed through the stages of eliminating manual labour (mechanisation) and reducing the demand for manual skill (machine tools, especially with numerical control) to the reduction of demand for routine mental exercise. This last stage is properly called automation, the essence of which is information handling.

The title of this book refers to *robots* whereas this chapter and the next refer to *automation*: how are the two related? To the layman the word 'robot' usually implies 'mechanical man' and this is supported etymologically by its origin in Capek's 1920's play 'Rossum's Univers-al Robots'. It is interesting to note that Capek coined the name from a Czech word meaning 'forced labour' and so a truly English equiva-lent might be based on 'galley slave'. The notion is of something which works unceasingly; and whereas the wretched human who is being subjected to forced labour has to continue to work in spite of becoming tired, the robot works untiringly as well as unceasingly. There are many mechanical devices which can be involved in eliminating human intervention from industrial production and which collectively constitute automation; but it does not follow that all of them, or indeed any, are robots. An obvious example of automation which does not involve robots is the machine for making electric light bulbs which was mentioned on p.36. A more controversial question is the status of the 'pick-and-place' device e.g. a press loader or unloader. The former repeatedly picks a single sheet of metal from a stack and places it in a press, which then closes to form the desired article. On the other side of the press an unloader can take out the formed pressing and deliver it either to a stack or to a conveyor of finished pressings. Table 8 shows the numbers of industrial robots in various countries in December, 1981, with Japan having nearly 45% of the total. It has been suggested, however, that the very large number in Japan includes pick-and-place devices. This table was compiled by the British Robot Association and quoted in the *Times* of 10th February 1982; and on 12th February the *Times* reported that USSR (which is not included in Table 8) hoped to have 12,000 industrial robots by the end of 1985. It was hoped that the number of robots in the U K would pass 2,000 in 1983 but the indications are that most of them will be of either American, Japanese or Italian origin. Apart from the American firm of Unimation, which was a successful pioneer in the design and manufacture of robots, most of the interested companies in Europe and America are seeking arrangements for the manufacture of robots of Japanese design.

Whether or not they are included in Table 8, pick-and-place devices might be classed as 'Detroit automation' because they perform repeatedly a small fixed cycle of operations. In a 1962 book [17] the author drew a distinction between 'Detroit automation', meaning mechanisms which work on a simple repetitive cycle, and 'cybernetic automation' in which the operation was modified, without human intervention, by the feedback of information arising within the system. In this sense the first generation of robots are not cybernetic — they work to a more or less pre-determined program. But the feature which distinguishes these robots from the pick-and-place devices is a certain measure of complexity of the operating cycle and *adaptability*. In practice this means that the robot can be 'taught' a

Country	Number of robots
Japan	10,000
USA	5,000
West Germany	2,300
Sweden	1,700
UK	713
France	600
Italy	450
Other Western counries	1,500

The number of industrial robots in various countries in December 1981, as estimated by the British Robot Association and quoted in the *Times.*

Table 8

complicated cycle of operations, which it then stores in an electronic memory, and when that program is no longer required it can be 'taught' a different one. It is these powers of learning and of memory which give the robot an anthropomorphic aspect, but it is only the second generation of robots, those with sensors of one kind or another, that will fulfil the above definition of 'cybernetic' and make the robot an effective replacement for the human worker.

It was said above that one should avoid anthropomorphic, Heath Robinson-like, schemes. So what about robots, which have usually been regarded as 'mechanical men'? There is nothing wrong in copying in a machine certain useful features of the human body. Most robots have a fixed base about which they can pivot more easily than a man can pivot about a fixed spot, an extensible arm which can reach any point in a specified volume of space, a 'wrist' which can pivot about either one or more axes and a 'hand' or gripper which can seize objects for which it is designed: the 'hand' might be only a fork for lifting certain objects, or a suction device for lifting light objects. These first generation robots — say from 1960 to the late 1970's — worked on a fixed cycle and could be likened to a one-armed man having none of the five senses and no brain other than memory. The human attribute possessed in some measure by the robots, in contrast to transfer machines, is *adaptability* — the ability (within limits) to be re-trained for a new task when the current task is no longer required. They have hitherto been mostly mimic or 'train and follow' devices which are led through a sequence of operations by a human operator and then can repeat the same sequence ad infinitum. Typical early applications were unloading metal bars from a furnace — where the surroundings would be unpleasant for a human operator — and manipulating a paint spray gun repetitively in front of a series of identical parts to be painted. More recently the most important application of robots has been for spot welding in automobile assembly. The presence of interlocks in the program, to ensure that the weld occurs at the right place and time, suggest the use of computer technique since computers are essentially logic machines. The robot may also be programmed to follow a work-piece moving along the assembly line. These features and the possibility of using digital memory now that silicon-chip memories with 64,000 bits capacity are becoming commonplace, are the main connections between advanced robots and silicon chips. More recently there has been a move to program robots 'off line', i.e. by feeding a program into the robot's computer instead of making it record human operations, and a programming language for this purpose has been named Rapt. This has two advantages. Firstly it does not require a human operator to intrude into the production line, with interruption of the production process. Secondly, 'train and follow' results in any hesitations or other weaknesses in the human performance being repeated ever after. So robots should be computer driven, rather than rely on in-built memory.

The current endeavour, still in the experimental stage in 1983, is to provide the robot with *senses*. The first, tactile, so that the pressure of the grip can be adjusted to a desired value, and the second, visual, so that the 'hand' can be positioned as required for the current work-piece instead of blindly following a program. The case for using robots rather than special-purpose machines is the greater flexibility of a computer-controlled device, both in carrying out a task and in the ability to be re-programmed for a new task when a production run has been completed. Moreover a mass-produced robot could be cheaper than a special-purpose machine designed and built in small numbers for a particular task.

One thinks that it is robots that are making the unmanned (or unwomanned?) factory a practical possibility. But it should first be mentioned that a largely automated mode of operation using an automatic machining centre named 'System 24' was demonstrated some years ago[9] by the British firm of Molins who made it. For this the work-pieces, e.g. castings to be machined, were attached to pallets; and enough pallets could be loaded during the day shift for the automatic machining centre to continue working through 24 hours. An installation consisting of, for example, six automatic machining centres would be supervised by a central computer which controlled the supply of parts to the operators loading the pallets, the supply of pallets to each machining centre, and the operations performed by the latter. This project was abandoned, one reason given being that 'it was before its time'. There were also practical limitations:

(i) It required a considerable day-shift labour force for loading the pallets.

(ii) It did not undertake assembly of finished piece-parts, and therefore could not automate the whole production process.

(iii) It has been said that the particular tools incorporated in the machining centres were appropriate only to certain materials. (This last is in fact a difficulty which could be easily overcome.)

None the less, the 'System 24' was very similar to the 'FMS' (Flexible Machining System) unit machining centres which are now being imported from Japan. This seems to be yet another case of 'invented in Britain but commercialised abroad'. The unit FMS centres are usually fed with loaded pallets; but a factory near Colchester which has recently been built by the 600 Group uses an arrangement called SCAMP FMS, which is more advanced in three respects. Firstly, the nine machining centres are served by eight robots which remove the blank or part-finished item from its transport pallet and insert it appropriately into the machining centre. Secondly, material on pallets (either raw material or part-finished items) is handled by a computer-controlled conveyor system which takes the pallet to the appropriate machining centre, with a queuing system in case this is already occupied. Thirdly, the machining centres in the SCAMP system can handle any machining operation, e.g. hobbing (gear cutting), whereas the unit FMS centres are usually limited to round or prismatic shapes of work. This is because the robot in SCAMP removes the work–piece from its pallet and can load it on to a spindle in the machining centre.

In fact the most difficult part of manufacture to automate is *assembly*. One of the most difficult things for a robot to do is to thread a nut on to a bolt! In the automobile industry there appears to be a division between *manufacture* and *assembly* which is not always recognised. On the 'assembly line' the problem of assembly in the nut–and–bolt sense is minimised by using welding for the joining of most metal parts; but the engine, which comes to the assembly line as a single complete unit, is itself an assembly of very many separate parts. It is comparatively easy to assemble a stack of parts on a shaft, and an example of the assembly of the armature parts for electric motors was reported in 1978.[10] The difficulty is in securing sufficiently exact placement of parts, especially when clearances are small. In this connection there was a Japanese robot hand, called the 'Hi–T hand',[11] which incorporated a controlled degree of flexibility and so was able to 'feel its way' in inserting a piston into a close–fitting cylinder, a task which it could perform more rapidly than a human operator. It is reported that in Japan there is experimental work on 'assembly cells', unit combinations of robots and so on, which will do for assembly what the FMS unit does for machining. The whole topic of FMS was the subject of a Conference[15] in October 1982 which has been reviewed[16] in January 1983.

The era of the (largely) unmanned factory is now upon us through the use of robots. In a remarkable paper which was privately circulated in April 1976, Dr. M.E.H. Larcombe of Warwick University warns that the next stage of automation would be the robot factory, that Japan looked likely to be foremost in this development and that several other countries appeared to be making more progress than the UK.[‡]

In Europe, Fujitsu Fanuc and Siemens in a 50–50 partnership are reported[12] to be planning to set up a factory run by robots in Luxembourg. It will employ 5 workers and 3 managers (i.e. only 5% of the usual work–force) and have 20 times the productivity of a conventional factory. It is also reported that the Yamazaki machine tool company has an 'unmanned' plant in Japan which employs six persons on each of two shifts and none on the third, whereas a conventional plant would need 250 on each of three shifts. The managing director is reported as saying,[13]

'We have had many enquiries from Britain and other parts of Europe. A large delegation of European representatives is coming to inspect our plant next month but we are too busy dealing with the American market at the moment'.

The alarming feature is to find Britain (and other parts of Europe) at the end of a queue to buy in Japan what we have failed to make ourselves. But there is just one gleam of hope. The British branch of Texas Instruments, one of the manufacturers of the 'silicon chips', is organising a number of 'System Integrator' companies[14] which will buy unpackaged microprocessors from Texas Instruments and sell automated systems to industrial companies. From their point of view it is presumably of secondary importance whether the robots which they install are of British or foreign manufacture; and from a national point of view it is probably more important that robots should be used by British industry than that they should be made in Britain.

Having been told about 'automation' and 'robots' the reader may be wondering about 'information technology', a term which has come to prominence following the recent Year of Information Technology, IT82. 'Information technology' is by definition concerned with the collection, transmission, storage and manipulation of information but *not* with its use. Thus IT covers advanced telecommunication systems (including cable television), computers and word processors but not automation or robots. This is something of an anomaly, for if one takes the popular misconception that IT is synonymous with 'chips with everything', then one notes that robots depend on chips for their operation and control. To this extent robots appear to depend on IT, but the usual definition of IT excludes these applications in productive industry, even though the importance there of the information–handling aspect of automation has long been recognised.[17] There is therefore an unfortunate tendency for IT to be associated firstly with computers (including word processors, data bases and the 'electronic office') and secondly with communication systems (including advanced telephone networks like 'System X' and international calls via satellites or cable television). Robots depend upon the combination of the concept established by Shannon,[4] that information is an entity which can be handled by physical systems, with the concept of feedback which may be loosely described in human terms as giving the ability to modify one's action in accordance with results already achieved. The principle of feedback is not new. James Watt's centrifugal governor is generally taken as its first engineering application and it was the basis of the 'servo' or 'automatic control' technology which has received considerable attention since 1945. One of the early applications was to the slewing of naval guns, but most of the technology employed at that time was based on the rotating machines of electric power engineering, with a minimum use of electronics. The combination of these two concepts is called cybernetics. From the point of view of production industry, therefore, Information Technology is of secondary importance. The need of first importance is to realise and utilise the power of *microelectronics* both in cybernetics (e.g. in robots) and in simplifying the operation of all kinds of machines (including consumer–oriented devices like washing machines and sewing machines). It is microelectronics which has made practical the advancement of automation to a new stage, since cybernetics has been known and explored for over 30 years.

This chapter has reviewed the development of automation, some of the techniques now available and the reduction in labour content of manufacture which is now possible. The general impact on employment will be discussed in Chapter 5.

NOTES

* The manufacture by Boulton of Watt's steam engines at a later date was also carried out at Soho.

** The situation in the service sector is still a mixture of wage employment and entrepreneurship.

† The difference is that the program for the NC machine tool is prepared 'off line' on an independent computer and 'read' later by an attachment to the machine tool, whereas the CNC machine tool is directly controlled by the computer.

†† Some manual micrometers have a rachet device on the knob which may be used to turn the screw, so that the maximum pressure is limited.

‡ Dr. Larcombe postulated that the addition of sensing to robots would make them cheaper, by reducing the required accuracy of mechanical construction because they could home in on a target position by sensing instead of relying on dead reckoning. He argued that the reduction in price and consequent wider use would grow cumultively. It is not clear that the addition of sensing has in fact been important in recent developments.

References

1. Charles Singer, E.J. Holmyard, A.R. Hall and Trevor J. Williams, *A History of Technology.* Clarendon Press, Oxford, 1957. (volume III, pp. 151—2).

2. S. Lilley, *'Automatic Factories', Discovery*, vol. 16, pp. 147—152, April 1955.

3. D.A. Bell, *Information Theory and its Engineering Applications* (4th. edn.) Pitman, London, 1968.

4. C.E. Shannon, 'A Mathematical Theory of Communication', *Bell Syst. Tech. Journal.* vol. 27, pp. 379—423 and 623—656, 1948.

5. A.J. Cronshaw, W.B. Heginbotham and A. Pugh, 'A Versatile Microcomputer Controlled Parts Feeding System', *Robots 79 Conference*, British Robot Association, March 1979.

6. Anon., 'Two Glass-blowing Monsters make 1,500,000 Bulbs a Day', *Discovery*, vol. 13, pp. 250—253, August 1952.

7. J. Deketh, *Fundamentals of Radio-valve Techniques.* London. Cleaver Hume, 1950.

8. Anon. 'Automatic Receiver Production', *Wireless World*, vol. 53 pp. 122—123, April 1947.
9. D.T.N. Williamson, 'Integrated Manufacturing Control', *Control Engineering*, September 1967, pp. 67—71.
10. Anon., 'Production Line for the Manufacture of Armatures for Universal Motors', *Automation*, May 1978, p. 33.
11. T. Goto, T. Inoyama and K. Takeyasu, 'Precise Insert Operation by Tactile Controlled Robot', Paper No. C1, *2nd. Conference on Industrial Robot Technology*, International Fluidics Services, Carlton, Bedford, England, March 1974.
12. Anon., 'Fujitsu Fanuc Automates Factory', *Computing*. 22nd October 1981, p. 13.
13. Peter Hazelhurst, 'Japanese Robots find Friends in the West', *The Times*, 17th November 1981, p. 6.
14. Anon., 'Texas Automates the Factory Floor', *Computing*, 15th October 1981.
15. *Proceedings of the 1st International Conference on Flexible Manufacturing Systems*. IFS Publications, Bedford: 1982.
16. Lewis Holmes, Computers in mechanical components manufacture. *Electronics & Power*, vol. 29, pp. 22-25, January 1983.
17. D.A. Bell, *Intelligent Machines*. London: Pitman, 1962.
18. Norbert Wiener, *Cybernetics: or control and communication in the animal and the machine*. New York: Wiley 1948.

Chapter 4

THE ECONOMICS OF AUTOMATION

Full automation, in the sense of eliminating all human workers from the productive process (although a few maintenance and ancillary persons are still required), is the culmination of a continuing progress from (human) labour-based industry to machine-based industry. In the intermediate state of this progress (say from 1946 to 1980) the tendency has been to regard the capital investment in machinery per employee in manufacturing industry in terms of assistance to the human worker, e.g. to discuss how many horsepower each worker has at his disposal. It is often suggested that British industry already suffers from employing less capital equipment per worker than some of its foreign competitors; but though this may well be true for particular industries, it is a very difficult point to establish in general. Figures collected by F.E. Jones[1] for the steel industry show that for the year ended 29th March 1980 fixed assets per employee in the British Steel Corporation averaged £9,166 after depreciation (188,000 employees) but £36,691 in a combined group of eight Japanese steel companies (222,844 employees). But 'fixed assets' includes land and buildings — see Chapter Note 1. One pointer to the value of machinery alone is an assumption of a life of 10 years for machinery and therefore a total stock of 10 times the annual expenditure on machinery.* A life of 10 years is commonly assumed for accounting purposes (valuation after depreciation to be shown in the balance sheet) but it is believed that much machinery in British industry is more than 10 years old. The 10-year basis would therefore tend to *under*-estimate the total existing stock of machinery. (See also Chapter Note 2).

The value of equipment per worker varies with the type of industry. For example, a small number of persons can operate an oil refinery costing millions of pounds, and Central Statistical Office (CSO) figures[2] for 1980 on the basis of 10-year expenditure lead to an average of £76,000 per employee in coal and petroleum production; but at the other extreme the 'textile, leather and clothing' industry averages little over £3,000 of plant per employee. In 1982 the average for all manufacturing industry in UK was estimated at £8,500 per employee for plant and equipment. Since there will be some assets in land and buildings, and something is required for working capital, this is consistent with the rule of thumb that the creation of a job costs £10,000. For example, a grant to N. Ireland in January 1982 of £90 million was expected to create 9,000 new jobs.) Expenditure by UK manufacturing industry on plant and machinery in constant 1975 prices has been fairly stable at about £2.8 billion p.a. from 1974 to 1980. More recent figures on fixed capital expenditure in manufacturing industry from 1978 onward[3] are available in constant 1980 prices. In these terms the annual expenditure reached a maximum in 1979 and fell to 60% of that value in 1982. The first quarter of 1983 (adjusted for the average seasonal variation between quarters) is the lowest yet, but the second and third quarters of 1983 show slightly higher investment, though less than in the corresponding quarters of 1982. What is certain, however, is that the capital investment per employee in the manufacturing industry will have to be enormously increased as industry moves towards the unmanned facory. Over the 10 years 1970 to 1979, the number of employees in the manufacturing industry fell by 18% (the total of those engaged in civil employment of all kinds fell by only 2½%) while output rose by over 7%. The switch of labour from manufacturing to other industries was beginning.

The Statistical Abstract of the USA[4] gives a figure for the stock of plant and equipment in the manufacturing industry in 1978 which leads to an estimate of £5,380 per worker. A more recent estimate[12] is $25,000 per worker. For Japan there is a figure available [15] for total orders for *machinery* from the manufacturing industry. One can arrive at an estimate of £5,000 per employee in the manufacturing industry. In comparison the average of the whole manufacturing industry in Britain on the same basis, would be £3,440. (See Chapter Note 3 for details of the US and Japanese figures.)

While industry has been regarded as labour based, 'productivity' has been defined as output per worker, regardless of the amount of capital employed. An index of *production* (volume, not value) is published by the CSO, as are figures for the numbers of employees in manufacturing. From these two one can derive an index of *productivity*, as detailed in Chapter Note 4. Taking the basis that productivity in 1970 equalled 100, the index of productivity showed a rising trend to a maximum of 135 in 1979 but fell to 131 in 1980. The index of the number of employees in manufacturing industry meanwhile fell steadily from 100 in 1970 to 82 in 1980, (see Chapter Note 4 for detailed figures). A consequence of the definition of productivity as output per worker is the idea that profits from productivity are prima facie the property of the workers i.e. there is the expectation of a wage increase related to productivity. (A further argument in this direction, whether expressed or only implied, is that the remaining workers should be financially compensated for the loss of job security implied by a reduction of the work-force in their particular occupation). Pressure to direct the gains from productivity to the local labour force militates against a reduction in price of the product which would both benefit a wider section of the community and improve the competitive position of the firm. But now that there is expectation that a robot-controlled factory will require only 5% of the labour force that would be required in an old-fashioned factory, perhaps the obvious lack of credibility of attributing the consequent 20:1 increase in 'productivity' to the labour force will put an end to this element of 'productivity bargaining' in wage negotiations.

It is sometimes suggested that the labour displaced from the production process, or an equivalent amount of other labour,** will be employed in the manufacture of the automation equipment, but this is manifestly incorrect. An essential condition for the introduction of automation is a reduction in overall cost. But the cost of the new equipment has in the past included on the one hand a large labour cost in design and development and on the other hand the cost of skilled labour in manufacture. In addition there is the capital cost of the plant making the equipment, marketing costs and an element of profit. If the cost of all this, averaged over the life of the equipment, is less than the cost of the less-skilled labour displaced, then the average number of persons employed must be much less than the number displaced. This statement was qualified by 'in the past', when robots and so forth were produced in small numbers. But increasing volume of production reduces the relative weight of design and development cost per unit and the Japanese company Fujitsu Fanuc now has a factory in which robots are manufactured by robots. Since this eliminates most of the labour involved in the manufacture of robots, it will be true a fortiori that the new labour force will be much smaller than that displaced.

What has just been demonstrated is that the use of labour–saving equipment in manufacturing industry reduces the overall demand for labour, measured simply as a number of persons. The activity of manufacturing automation equipment or robots does create some new jobs, but they will be of higher skill status than those lost, with an increasing proportion of 'white collar' jobs in R & D (Research and Development) and in administration. This will be discussed further in Chapter 5. When considering the possible advantages to a manufacturer of reducing the labour force, one must recognise that there may be at least three factors involved:

1. Reduction of labour cost, including on–costs such as National Insurance, pension, holiday pay, sick pay and the cost of personnel management and administration together with canteen and other welfare expenditure. All these together may add 30% to the wage bill.

2. Elimination of unreliability due to sickness or strikes (the reliability of robots should be ensured by systematic 'preventive maintenance').

3. Overcoming shortage of *skilled* labour.

In relation to 'welfare' in (1) it is also suggested that robots do not need the same standard of heating, lighting and ventilation as human workers. This is contrary to experience with computers which demand a very high standard of air-conditioning with temperature and humidity control. But robots are engineering machines and designed to work in an ordinary factory environment; and so they may be more tolerant than human workers — in fact one of their first applications was to handling hot metal parts in conditions which the human worker would find unpleasant or intolerable.

In addition to the desire to reduce the labour force, there may be other motives for introducing automation:

1. To achieve results which would be impossible by manual methods.

2. To obtain greater output from a given factory area. (This applies especially to Japan, where space is very limited).

3. To reduce the investment in work in progress.

The integrated circuit or 'silicon chip' is a good example of the use of machines, including computers, to carry out tasks which are beyond the capabilities of human hands and brains. The current commercial effort in Large Scale Integration (LSI) is the manufacture of memories of over 64,000 'bits'[†] capacity.

Apart from the general utility of large memories — the storage capacities of large computers are now measured in megabytes — the memory unit is the first target of advanced silicon-chip techniques because it is simple in structure: all of the 64,000 elements are identical and they are uniformly arranged in rows and columns with uniform connections. But the chip which contains the greater part of a microprocessor has to accommodate different elements in various positions and a specific arrangement of the necessary interconnections between them. LSI has been likened[13] to a map of Southern England having throughout the fineness of detail of a London street map which shows individual blocks of buildings; and VLSI would extend the map to half Western Europe. Such an extensive and complex array is beyond the capabilities of the human intellect and is designed by computer, according to programs which are, of course, of human origin. The human brain determines the principles, but the computer carries out the detailed work. The reduction of the design to microscopic size on a silicon chip no more than a centimetre square is carried out mechanically, originally using photographic methods but now increasingly using either X-rays or electron beams to overcome the problem of diffraction which limits the fineness of detail possible with visible light. There is a great deal of both capital equipment and investment of man-years in the original design. But once everything has been designed and the manufacturing equipment set up, the cost of producing additional chips is comparatively small — hence the cheap home computer.

There is a final stage of manufacture which is still carried out to some extent by hand. Various points on the silicon-chip circuit must be joined to externally accessible contacts to which connections can be made and the chip must be enclosed in a capsule (often of plastic) for mechanical protection and protection against moisture etc. These operations of final assembly are commonly performed in a location of low labour cost, e.g. Taiwan. No doubt these operations too will be fully automated if low cost labour ceases to be available.

One of the ancillary claims for automation is that it reduces capital tied up in work in progress: an extreme claim from Japan[6] is that work can be completed in two days after complete automation, whereas it used to take three months. Recent high interest rates in the West have caused great emphasis — perhaps excessive emphasis — to be placed on this factor. (See Chapter Note 5 for further discussion.)

Traditionally the main impediment to automation has been the large capital expenditure involved, which could be tolerated only by large–scale enterprises when there were expectations of a market for a large volume of output. The 'large volume' implied a consumer product for which there were millions of customers (or many millions if one aimed at an international market). The typical example has been the automobile industry, where the capital cost of a production line has been extremely high. This industry has been sustained by 'built in obsolescence' of which there have been two factually identifiable constitutents:

(a) There are some genuine improvements in the product from time to time.

(b) There has been a tendency for rust to limit the life of a vehicle unless special precautions had been taken by the purchaser. (To be fair, manufacturers have been made aware of this problem and are now (1984) taking precautions during manufacture.)

Consumer markets tend to saturate. (One could have a television receiver in every room in the house, but who wants several washing machines?) and the reaction to this has been to switch to a new product. This surely leaves a market niche for someone who is able to manufacture efficiently items in smaller quantities for the replace-ment market. Within the electronics industry we have seen the progression from radio to television (but with a minor revival of radio in the portable transistorised form, together with the portable cassette player, and as a constituent of hi–fi music centres), from 405 to 625 line television and from black–and–white to colour. Videotext (Ceefax, Oracle, Prestel) does not look like achieving a mass market, so the next major move may be to TV games coupled with home computers or to video recorders. Examples of completely new products are the ball pen, the pocket electronic calculator, TV games and the video recorder. A question mark still hangs over satellite and cable television. What next? Well, the person who can give the right answer ought to make a fortune, but one who acts on the wrong answer may lose one!

It has long been traditional for automation to be considered feasible only for large-scale production in units employing large numbers (at least, before automation). At the same time it is widely held that good industrial relations are in practice achieved best in unit establisments of not more than 300 — 400 employees; and there is also a need for some products in only limited quantities. It is therefore important for automation to be extended to smaller units. The National Engineering Laboratory worked out a scheme[7] with the example of the replacement of 100 conventional machine tools in a batch production workshop having 60 employees by an automatic multi-purpose machining centre which would cost up to £1.8 million at 1977 prices and require the employment of a total of 21 persons. (This allowed for working three shifts, with triplication of some jobs.) In comparison with the conventional workshop this offered a gain of nearly 3:1 in both numbers employed and length of time of the production cycle. It had the disadvantage of 'putting all one's eggs in one basket' in the form of a large capital investment, but even so, claimed to produce a financial saving. Arrangements of this kind are now known as Flexible Manufacturing Systems and the present-day FMS machining centre, capable of storing programs for machining any of 11 different work-pieces, costs less than £100,000.

In the past, and to some extent even now, the price of robots must have included a large element of overheads to cover the costs of design and development, as well as any capital costs for their manufacture in small numbers. If the price can be reduced sufficiently — e.g. by the Fujitsu Fanuc company's development of the manufacture of robots by robots — it becomes practicable to associate robots with ordinary machinery used in a small workshop. It has been reported that this already happens in Japan[6] where robots can be leased so cheaply that in one case a very small plastic-moulding business replaced all three of its workshop employees by robots, to become literally a one-man business (though his wife provided occasional assistance while the proprietor was out playing golf!).

It is often said that high interest rates deter investment, whether by a user investing in the purchase of a robot or by a manufacturer investing in the holding of a stock of robots which are leased out. But in recent years the minimum interest rate in the UK, either the minimum lending rate (MLR) fixed by the Government or more recently the base lending rate of commercial banks, has been small or even negative *after allowing for inflation* (as evidenced by the success of indexed National Savings). It has therefore been quite economically sound for a firm to make a capital investment *provided* it could both sell its output at a continuing profit i.e. at a price rising with inflation, and remain in business for a few years. Periodical reviews of British Industry (by Financial Times and by CBI) have shown that it is lack of confidence in future sales and profit, rather than lack of finance, that has deterred capital investment. There is also the problem whether the introduction of robots or other automatic machinery should be regarded as replacement of old machinery or as new investment. The former should be paid for out of retained profits, but the latter justifies raising new capital, i.e. long–term borrowing, if the firm cannot meet the cost from internal funds. (Depreciation is further discussed in Chapter Note 6.)

There would be little point in quoting specific figures which are liable to change from year to year with inflation and which may differ widely in different countries with regards to their native labour costs. However, one *can* state general relationships. If the purchase of a robot is regarded as an investment then the annual cost, consisting of interest on capital and depreciation, might be 30% of the capital value. (This is taking present nominal UK interest rates and disregarding inflation.) The direct labour force in an unmanned factory is typically reduced to 5% of its previous number, but is more highly skilled so that the wage bill might only be reduced to 7½% of its original cost. Furthermore, the total cost to the employer of each employee will be more than just the nominal wage. Putting all this together with an estimate of the capital cost of a robot, the annual cost of a robot appears to be comparable with the annual cost of one human worker (in Britain in 1983). But the pay-off comes from the fact that the human worker reckons to work only 40 hours per week whereas the robot can work 160 hours and still leave a full 8–hour shift for maintenance or change of program. If the firm is already working three shifts per 24 hours, then there is no question because the robot replaces three operators. But if the firm is working only one or two shifts, the question is whether either sales could be greatly expanded to absorb additional production or the plant could be scaled down so that three–shift working with robots would produce the same output as the previous single–shift working. There is the further possibility that if robots are cheap enough they might be worked only for a single shift, so that the small amount of human supervision required could also work only a single shift. This may already be happening in small enterprises in Japan. Choice between the three possibilities will depend on local circumstances, though there is a general argument against unlimited expansion, which will be discussed below.

If present direct–labour costs amount to 40% of total costs,[††] change to robots could result in a 30% reduction in total costs (allowing a little for secondary effects such as reduction in work in progress and in finished stock). One can then see why it will be difficult for an old–fashioned firm to compete with a robot factory. The effect will be compounded by two factors:

(a) inflation tends to reduce the total cost of capital expenditure for the future,
(b) the long–term trend is for wages to rise relative to other costs.

The latter effect is already apparent in Japan.

The above argument applies directly to the setting up of a new factory, but it must be emphasised that the conversion of an existing factory is fraught with difficulties, including the fate of the displaced labour, so that the widespread introduction of robots will take a considerable time. Nevertheless, the introduction of robots by one manufacturer in a particular trade at any time (possibly not in Britain) will be a serious threat to all its competitors.

It was mentioned above that consumer markets tend to saturate. In addition there is a kind of 'Gresham's law'[‡] that the existence of a cheap product of whatever quality tends to destroy the market for an expensive equivalent of high quality, even though overall the latter may be better value for money.

A related problem is that in times of inflation consumers endeavour to obtain a corresponding increase in income but still object to increased prices. A factor which is particularly relevant to employment is that the cost of labour has increased so much more than the cost of sophisticated mass–produced articles (cars, television receivers, quartz–controlled digital watches) that there is great reluctance to employ labour for more or less personal services (house decorating, gardening, laundry etc.) and together with increased leisure this has led to a boom in 'DIY' At the same time there is a shortage of skilled labour in many service trades.

A fundamental limit on expansion is the global limitation of resources of raw materials, including energy.[10&11] Taking the last item first, every industrial process involves some expenditure of energy, while some, such as the manufacture of steel or fertilisers, require a great deal. Oil has been the most favoured source of energy for several decades; but since 1973 the price of oil has been increased steeply, mainly by the action of the OPEC producers, and there is also anxiety as to how long supplies will last. (It *always* seems to be estimated at 20—30 years from now!) Efforts are therefore made to reduce the consumption for all purposes but a moderate increase in industrial output is not inconsistent with restraint on energy use. For example, statistics of the nine early members of the Common Market[8] show that the energy per unit volume of product decreased from a base of 100 in 1970 to 82 in 1977 (statistics are not available for later years). Another example is that the British Steel Corporation in 1982 consumed an energy of 22 gigajoules (GJ) for every ton of liquid steel it produces, compared with 32 GJ some years ago.[9] Nonetheless there are complaints from industries which must use large amounts of energy that relative costs of energy in different countries and to different users vary to the detriment of competitivity and hence employment in their own enterprises. For example, the British Steel Corporation, which has drastically reduced its labour force, is dissatisfied with the price it pays for bulk electrical energy which it uses in the electric arc and induction furnaces for making special steels. There has also been a trend for tinplate (i.e. steel sheet thinly plated with tin) in 'tins' to be replaced by aluminium for packaging in, for example, beer cans. But the production of aluminium metal necessarily requires a very large expenditure of energy (see Chapter Note 7 for the chemistry of this). It has traditionally been associated with hydroelectric schemes, but even so there has been public objection (in New Zealand) to the low price of bulk supplies to an aluminium refinery. It seemed an ideal base load for a nuclear power station, but at the beginning of 1982 a venture of this kind at Hunterston in Scotland was declared to be uneconomic. A great deal of aluminium has been used in buildings in recent years and the energy content of various materials (i.e. the energy consumed in the production of the usable material from natural resources) is an important consideration in their large–scale use.

Other resources, besides energy, are limited in quantity. A US estimate in the 1970's implied that supplies of copper would barely last until the end of the century[‡‡]   and of aluminium less than 100 years from then, though a later US survey of world resources[11] found no shortage of non–fuel minerals up to the year 2000. There is also concern over the increasing use of paper for ephemeral purposes in both packaging and communication. The large–scale destruction of forests to provide timber and paper is causing soil erosion, changes in climate and other ecological problems.

The rising price of oil is one form of the limitation on the use of energy. In industrialised countries it leads to a struggle between incomes and prices, each individual trying to pass off the additional fuel cost to the community through higher wages or higher prices for his products and in so doing increasing inflation. In the less-advanced countries which do not have indigenous oil resources, oil is often a major, even dominant, item in external trade. An increase in the price of oil may mean a reduction in volume of other imports, even of food, with consequent fall in an already meagre standard of living.

Although oil is the most publicised factor, and the one on which there has been the most obvious pressure both of price and of expected shortage, other resources must be watched. Aluminium and copper have already been mentioned and it is probably fortunate that microelectronics moved from germanium to silicon, because the former is a comparatively scarce material. The eventual obtaining of power from nuclear fusion (the 'hydrogen bomb' effect) seems at present likely to depend on the availability of lithium just as much as the present nuclear fission depends on uranium (see Chapter Note 8).

In summary, the limitation of natural resources implies that the introduction of automation will inevitably be aimed mainly at a reduction in labour force for comparable or modestly increased output (perhaps doubled) rather than at an unlimited increase in output from the same labour force. That is to say, there will be a decrease in employment rather than an increase in production. It therefore calls for a substantial transfer of labour from production industries either to service industries or to leisure in one form or another. Politicians of any party who believe that a mere increase in general economic activity (whether due to 'reflation' or to 'the end of the recession') would eliminate growing long–term unemployment, are ignoring the facts.

Notes for Chapter 4

Note 1. *Assets of the steel industry.*
The figures quoted by F.E. Jones are for *fixed assets*, which term includes land and buildings as well as plant and vehicles. (The latter two are usually combined, but in productive industry the part attributed to 'vehicles' is usually small compared with plant.) Another difficulty is that the valuation entered in the balance sheets used to be only that based on the historic cost method of accounting, i.e. the *original* purchase price less depreciation, though some companies re-value land and buildings at current market price from time to time. The accounts of BSC for the year 1980—81 show land and buildings valued at £286 million compared with £1411 million for plant etc., confirming that the latter is the larger part. Another difficulty in comparisons, particularly between countries having very different rates of inflation, is that old but still serviceable plant will have a low value on the historic cost basis where inflation is high. However, the absence of any additional depreciation under 'current cost accounting' (see Chapter Note 6) seems to rule out this effect in relation to BSC. The comparative figures quoted on p. 51 therefore still stand.

Note 2. *Fixed Assets in Britain.*
As noted in the text, expenditure by the manufacturing industry on plant has for a number of years been fairly steady at £2.8 billion at 1975 prices. In addition there has been about £1.2 billion p.a. on buildings. If one takes conventional depreciation lives of 10 years for plant and 40 years for buildings, this implies a total of £76 billions of fixed assets. But Table 14.21 of the 'Annual Abstract of Statistics' for 1982 gives an estimate of £105.1 billion for the replacement cost (at 1975 prices) of the gross fixed assets of manufacturing industry in 1980. One way of reconciling these two very different estimates would be to assume that the actual life of assets is longer than the nominal depreciation life. Casual observation suggests that buildings often remain in use for much longer that 40 years — perhaps a hundred years is more appropriate — and a survey shortly after the 1939—45 war alleged that many machine tools in British industry were more than 20 years old. More recent evidence is not to hand, but the weak

state of the British machine tool industry would be consistent with a reluctance of British industry to buy machine tools, though foreign competition is also a major factor. This illustrates the difficulty of arriving at any reliable estimate of plant employed per worker. The annual spending by various branches of industry may be as much an indication of the prosperity of each industry as of the amount of plant it posseses. The amount of depreciation entered in a company's accounts has often been influenced by the amount which the Inland Revenue will allow to be charged against pre-tax profit.

Note 3. *Equipment per worker in USA and in Japan.*
The 'Statistical Abstract of the USA'[4] gives figures for both net stock of manufacturing equipment and depreciation, at current prices and at constant 1972 prices. The ratio of stock to depreciation has remained fairly steady over the years 1960 to 1978 at about 7½:1, representing an effective life of equipment of 7½ years only. The valuation in 1980 at current prices of the net stock of manufacturing equipment was $381.4 billion and the corresponding employment 21.6 million, giving a value of $17,657 per employee, or at a rough figure of $2= £1 § a value of £8,800 per employee. This is comparable with the figure quoted in the text for Britain in 1980.

In Japan in 1981, orders from manufacturing industry for machinery amounted to 29,176 hundred million yen while employment in manufacturing industry was 13.85 million. This leads to a figure of 210,700 yen per employee, which at 421 yen = £1 is equivalent to an annual expenditure of £500 per employee. On a ten-year basis this would represent total capital of £5,000 per employee: this compares with the latest British figure of about £8,000 per employee.

Note 4. *Index of productivity.*
In its Monthly Digest of Statistics the CSO publishes an index of *production* which is intended to measure relative volume of output, independent of prices. It also publishes a figure for the number of employees, which excludes owners of businesses and workers on their own account (self-employed). There is some uncertainty about numbers employed, which were at first calculated from surveys of industry but later from counts of the numbers of National Insurance cards in circulation. One can then estimate an index of the size of the labour force, taking 1970 to equal 100, and dividing the production index by the labour force index gives a productivity index. The

figures for 1970 to 1980 so estimated are shown in the following table, for manufacturing industries in Great Britain.(Table 9.)

Two points deserve special note. Firstly, the fall in productivity between 1979 and 1980 means that employment did not fall as fast as output. Secondly, the total of those engaged in all forms of civil employment, including non–industrial employment and also including employers and the like, fell only (from an index of 100 in 1970) to 97.6 in 1980. All figures refer to Great Britain, i.e. England, Wales and Scotland but excluding N. Ireland.

Note 5. *On the cost of holding stock.*
The recent high interest rates have caused great emphasis to be placed on the cost of having money tied up in stock of all kinds. The amount necessarily embodied in work in progress varies with the kind of industry to fall somewhere between the extremes of ship–building, where the time to complete a job may be measured in years, and the food industry where perishable goods must reach the consumer as quickly as possible. A manufacturing firm in the engineering industry (to which robots appear most immediately applicable) may have a total stock (as shown in the balance sheet) valued at 30% of a year's sales; and this is usually divided fairly equally between the three categories of (a) raw matertials and fuel, (b) work in progress, and (c) stock of finished product. The minimum value of (a) depends essentially on the reliability of suppliers (and transport), though it may also be influenced by the economy of bulk purchase. A stock of finished product is held to ensure that customers' orders can be met within a reasonable time. Theoretically the size of this stock depends on the time for which the customer is expected to be willing to wait and the time taken to manufacture additional stock, but in practice it depends mainly on the accuracy with which sales can be forecast. Item (b) is directly reduced if automation speeds up production and it may be possible to reduce (c) if the manufacturing time is comparable with an acceptable customer waiting time. In that case, the stock of raw materials must be increased to provide a buffer against varying sales rates, but as this does not include the added value of manufacture, it should be cheaper than a stock of finished product. An extreme case has been quoted in which the manufacturing time in an engineering works was reduced by complete automation from three months to two days.[6] Allowing for some transfer from finished stock to raw materials, this might roughly halve the total investment

Year	Production	Labour Force	Productivity
1970	100.0	100.0	100.0
1971	100.3	96.3	104.2
1972	102.5	92.7	110.6
1973	110.0	93.9	117.1
1974	107.0	93.9	114.0
1975	101.7	89.0	114.3
1976	103.7	86.6	119.7
1977	107.6	87.8	122.6
1978	111.0	87.8	126.4
1979	115.2	85.4	134.9
1980	107.3	81.7	131.3

Table 9

in stock and so make a material contribution to profit.

Note 6. *Depreciation*.
The traditional method of accounting, now known as 'historic cost accounting', subtracted a fixed proportion of the value of assets each year. Usually it was a proportion of initial cost ('straight-line depreciation') and the total cost was typically spread over 10 years for machinery and 40 years or more for buildings. This implies that the corresponding proportion of the assets should be replaced or renewed every year: otherwise one should set up a sinking fund to recoup the whole value of assets after the set number of years. Inflation has made this method useless, since the replacement cost of the asset will be far higher than the original cost which appears in the accounts. The system known as current cost accounting (CCA) overcomes this by requiring an estimate of the *present* value of the assets, calculating depreciation on this basis and noting a figure for 'additional depreciation' i.e. additional to that derived from the historic cost of the assets. The present value of assets can therefore be estimated from the total depreciation under CCA. (It also makes certain other adjustments to the balance sheet: see glossary.)

Note 7. *Energy Requirement for Aluminium*.
Aluminium combines very strongly with oxygen. This characteristic is concealed from the ordinary user of aluminium metal by the fact that the metal is always covered by a transparent film of aluminium oxide which prevents further penetration of oxygen into the metal.
The preparation of metallic aluminium from its ores depends ultimately on breaking down this combination, which must always require a great deal of energy. The extraction of metallic aluminium from its ores is effected by electrolysis, so the energy is supplied in electrical form and the economic production of aluminium requires a cheap supply of electrical energy, which has traditionally been obtained from hydroelectric generators. The more recent suggestion of using nuclear energy arises from the concept of 'base load'. One of the problems of the electricity supply industry is that demand peaks in the morning and afternoon but is less in the evening and is very low between about midnight and 6 a.m. (It is also less in summer than in winter.) The problem was not so intolerable with coal or oil fuelled power stations, because fuel cost is about half their total cost of generating and can be controlled by shutting down power stations for

a few hours and re-starting them when needed. With nuclear power stations, on the other hand, the cost of fuel is small, most of the cost being in the capital investment in building the power station; and it is technically impossible to shut down a nuclear reactor for a short time and re-start it quickly. Therefore nuclear power stations should preferably supply power which is needed for 24 hours per day and 365 days per year: This is known as 'base load' on which are super-imposed the daily and seasonal peaks. The electrolytic extraction of aluminium is ideally suited to using electrical power continuously — as a base load.

Note 8. *Raw materials for nuclear energy.*
It is well known that production of nuclear energy by the first generation of nuclear reactors which work on nuclear fission requires a supply of uranium, sometimes enriched in the fissile isotope. These reactors, however, use only a part of the energy theoretically available from the uranium. The breeder reactor, in commercial use in France, but not yet in Britain, is able to use also the plutonium produced by the earlier reactors (which otherwise would only have been of military use) and thorium. Even so, the supply of uranium is lkely to be tight around the end of the 20th century.

Nuclear fusion — the 'hydrogen bomb' process — is not likely to be in use within this century. The present preferred procedure involves the use of lithium. The element lithium is quite common in the earth's crust, but extended facilities will be needed to extract metallic lithium from its ores.

NOTES

* This is sometimes called the 'perpetual inventory' method.

** 'other labour' would be more probable, because labour is in general resistant to change of occupation.

† 64 kilobits in computer terminology means $2^{16}q$ 65,536 bits.

†† This refers to the labour costs within any one establishment. But bought-in components and materials contain their own labour cost, so that two-thirds of the National Income is paid out in wages and salaries.

‡ Gresham's law was that bad money (forged or inflated) drives good money out of circulation.

‡‡ The use of copper, in the form of electrical parts of machinery is now so widespread that its presence in scrap steel, which must be used to start the melt in an electric induction furnace, is an embarrassment to the British Steel Corporation in its preparation of pure steel.

§ These are 1980 figures.

References

1. F.E. Jones, *Added value: the rules of the game including a look at some engineering companies*. Lecture published by the Engineering Industries Association, London 1980.
2. CSO *Monthly Digest of Statistics* November 1981, Tables 1.8 and 3.3 HMSO.
3. *Monthly Digest of Statistics*, November 1983, HMSO.
4. *Statistical Abstract of the USA*, US Government Printing Office, Washington DC, Annually.
5. *Economic Statistics of Japan 1980*. Bank of Japan, Tokyo.
6. 'TV Eye' programme on Japan. Thames Television, 11th February 1982.
7. *Automated Small-batch Production*. National Engineering Laboratory, 1978. HMSO.
8. *Energy Statistics 1973–77*. Statistical Office of the European Community, Luxembourg.
9. Iain Macgregor, lecture at Sheffield, 11th November 1981.
10. DH Meadows, *The Limits of Growth*. Signet, New York 1975.
11. *The Global 2,000 Report to the President*. Penguin, London, 1982.
12. Alvin Toffler, *The Third Wave*. Bantam books, New York 1980.
13. Dennis Moralee, Visions of the VLSI Future. *Electronics and Power*, vol.28 no.4, pp 301–305. April 1982.

Chapter 5

THE DESTRUCTION AND CREATION OF JOBS

The 'army of the unemployed' is not a constant group of persons but rather a 'reservoir' through which there is a flow: some poeple lose jobs, but others find new jobs. The number of unemployed rises when the rate at which jobs are lost exceeds the rate at which vacancies are filled; and since this is essentially a queuing process, it follows inevitably that the *duration of unemployment* increases in a time of increase in the *number of unemployed*. It is therefore very difficult to examine duration of unemployment as a separate factor. But intuitively it seems likely that if the average duration for a male under 40 reached 12 months, then, because of the way the labour market runs, for a male over 60 the average duration would reach 5 years, i.e. he would never work again. This would clearly be unsatisfactory, and illustrates why a very high rate of unemployment is unsatisfactory. Nevertheless, unemployment is basically a flow process with usually a finite duration for each individual. Unemployment is now so high compared with the 1950's that we are accustomed to thinking of it as an unmitigated evil which ought to be eliminated. But Beveridge[1] postulated firstly, that about 1% of the work–force seemed incapable of securing employment even in prosperous circumstances and secondly, that some additional unemployment was necessary in order to provide a reserve of labour from which new enterprises could draw their employees. In the absence of such a reserve, a new enterprise would have to entice employees away from existing enterprises by offering higher wages, or the equivalent in other benefits, others would have to follow suit to compete and this would lead to inflation of wages. This led to the definition of 'full employment' as an unemployment rate of 3%, including an allowance for seasonal workers, i.e. 97% employment. Some people look for 100% employment, while others speak of 'over–full employment' when the percentage of unemployment is low. In the USA 4% of unemployment is acceptable, while in Japan, 2% is regarded as inconsistent with full employment; but one of the difficulties in international comparisons is differences in the bases of the figures. When speaking of 'over-full employment' one must remember that there can be other causes of inflation besides wage pressure. Furthermore, it has long been held that a small but constant inflation rate — say 5% p.a. — is acceptable* and may in fact facilitate the smooth running of the economic system. What is certainly *not* acceptable is an inflation rate which increases from year to year, 5%, 10%, 15%, 20%.. and so on. The unemployment rate is associated with the general level of activity in the economy (one speaks of 'overheating' if the economy is pressed to too high a level of activity). Therefore when the term 'non-accelerating inflation rate' (NAIR) of unemployment is used[2] it means the rate of unemployment which overall is consistent with a modest and *constant* rate of general inflation. This may not be the same as the rate needed on 'Beveridge' grounds to avoid *wage* inflation (because of arguments related to 'overheating') and its amount is open to dispute. In this book unemployment will be considered only from the 'Beveridge' point of view. General fiscal policy is outside our scope, and there is political dispute as to whether unemployment is being used deliberately as a tool of government policy, rather than arising as a by-product of the current situation and policies which are being adopted for other reasons. Here we shall consider what jobs are likely to be destroyed, and what created, by mechanisms other than government fiscal policy.

The 'Beveridge' point of view, which indeed underlies the practices of the Manpower Services Commission, is that apart from the residue of perhaps 1% of 'unemployables' in the work-force, unemployment is temporary while the worker is moving from one job to another *of the same kind*. Thus a skilled engineering worker, e.g. a fitter and turner, might find a job of the same kind in any application of mechanical engineering such as manufacture of textile machinery, of railway locomotives or of food-processing machinery, to name a few random examples.

If there were a constant rate of loss of jobs and an equal rate of creation of new jobs the total number of unemployed would depend on *how long* they took to effect the transfer from one job to another. It has been questioned whether the unemployed are now too 'choosey' about finding new jobs and thus prolong unemployment unnecessarily. Apart from the question of expectations, which are influenced by the social and economic norms of the period, it could be suggested that the introduction in 1966 of a 6-month period of earnings–related unemployment benefit and of redundancy payments, encouraged delay in taking a new job; but there is no statistical evidence of this. The main feature is that it is usually no longer possible to move to another job *of the same kind* and this is likely to be even more difficult in the future. On the other hand, there are even now a certain number of vacancies for skilled or experienced workers which remain unfilled. One suspects that the corresponding 'frictional' unemployment is due to geographical immobility and that this in turn results partly from the extreme lack of rented accommodation in Britain. Private letting has been largely eliminated by legislation which favours tenants against landlords (security of tenancy, rent control measures in particular) and the present government is trying to reduce local–authority letting by the sale of council houses to tenants. Council letting has in any case always discouraged geographical mobility by a policy of priority for local applicants. There is also a strong cultural feeling, especially among manual workers, against 'breaking up communities' and requiring individuals to 'pull up their roots'. But in any case the fact remains that in the early 1980's the number of unemployed far exceeds the number of vacancies so that on the whole unemployment cannot be 'voluntary'.

The major difficulty is that new jobs which are being created are not like the jobs which are being lost. When a television factory is set up in a town where there are many unemployed steel workers, Bridgend, for example, one can forecast that apart from the question of numbers (e.g. 250 out of 7,000) most of the new employment will go to wives and daughters, not to the unemployed men. A recent survey of another steel town (Consett)[15] reports that 5,500 steel workers had been made redundant and knock-on effects had meant that a total of 7,000 jobs were lost. New industry provided 1,500 jobs and it is hoped that a further 1,500 jobs will arise from this over the next three years. This would leave 4,000 unemployed in 1986 in a town which had a *population* of 35,000: and if it followed the national average, the male work–force would probably be about 9,000. The provision of 3,000 jobs against the loss of 7,000 looks like solving nearly half the problem; but doubts arise when one reads the detailed description of one small element of the new industry, a computer firm. This has at present an entire staff of seven, of whom, only two are former BSC employees, a technician and an administrator — not manual workers.

Of course one cannot deduce from one small example that the majority of unemployed steel workers will not find employment in new industry, but conversely it does show that new high-technology industry does not always provide jobs for unemployed manual workers. The fact is that Britain has a number of basic industries left over from the industrial revolution (textiles, steel, ship-building) which must now compete with developing countries. This is especially relevant because the first steps toward industrialisation in developing countries have traditionally been to establish textile and steel indus-tries. Either we must modernise — 'automate' — and specialise to such an extent that our advantage in expertise outweighs the advantages of the newly-built factories and low work rates in developing countries or we must abandon these basic industries completely. The case of steel is exacerbated by the fact that there is in the early 1980's a decline in world demand for steel so that every steel-producing country is looking to maximise its exports and minimise its imports. The Prime Minister (Mrs. Thatcher) said at the IT 82 Conference that in Scotland the electronics industry provides more employment than the steel and shipbuilding industries. Yet a few weeks later the Government refused to allow the closure of the Ravenscraig steel works, knowing full well that unemployed steel workers would not find employment in the electronics industry. The problem of aptitude for training or re-training for different jobs will be considered in Chapter 6.

Table 10 shows a comparison between the numbers employed in various industries in 1971 and 1982. (Those shown in italics are included in the immediately preceding main heading.) One has to take a reasonably long span of years to show a definite trend. It may be argued that in 1982 the figures are depressed by the recession, but this will apply to all figures so that comparisons are still valid. This table illustrates the move from 'production' to 'service' industries as well as the reduction in overall employment. The latter is not as great as the current rate of unemployment because, (a) unemployment was already 3.5% in 1971 and (b) the work-force was larger in 1982 than in 1971. It is estimated below that higher economic activity ('the end of the recession') might reduce unemployment by about 4%. The industrial group of 'agriculture, forestry and fishing' is the only one which remained unchanged over the period.

This illustrates the continuing movement from goods-related to service-related employment. This is nothing to be ashamed of, and

	Thousands		% change
	June 1971	June 1982	
All employees	22,509	20,520	−8.9
All production industries	10,684	7,376	−30.7
Metal manufacture	*555*	*298*	*−46.7*
Textiles	*657*	*339*	*−48.4*
Food, drink and tobacco	*867*	*608*	*−29.0*
Catering, hotels	568	896	+57.7
Professional and scientific services	2,979	3,689	+23.8
Insurance, banking, finance	982	1,237	+26.0
Miscellaneous services	1,264	1,496	+18.4
National government	577	601	+4.2
Local government	880	956	+8.6

Change in numbers employed in various industries, June 1971 to June 1982.

Note: The service industries shared the general decline in *numbers* during 1980—82, but continued to show a slow increase in their percentage of total employment. During the first two quarters of 1983 the numbers in service industries also increased, though the numbers in manufacturing industry continued to decrease.

Table 10

some of the service industries produce valuable 'invisible' exports. However, the favourable balance of trade in such 'invisibles' is less than half the amount of the import bill for food alone. Therefore we cannot afford to ignore the export performance of goods–related production industries. The table does not, however, show the changes which are taking place within each production industry. An interesting consequence of the development of automatic machinery for the manufacture of electric light bulbs and radio valves was the complete elimination of one skilled job, namely that of 'stemmers, sealers and exhausters'. The primitive method of manufacture required that a worker skilled in glass–blowing should take the stem — a piece of glass tubing to one end of which the electrical components had already been attached — and seal it into the bulb, evacuate the bulb and then seal the bulb off at its point of connection to the vacuum pump. In the 1931 census there was a specific occupational heading 'Electric lamp and valve stemmers sealers and exhausters' (Order IX, code number 257) which listed 144 men and 1192 women. But in the 1951 census reports these could not be separately identified: there were only 'machine setters' (code number 235) and 'machine minders' (code number 236) under 'other production process workers' (nothing specifically related to lamps and valves). Thus what had once been a specific skilled occupation had ceased to exist.

Table 11 shows a cross–section on two different axes of change in the engineering industry. In (a) there is shown the slow change with time, over a period of ten years, in the whole of the engineering industry, the significant features being an increase in the percentages of the top two classes and a decrease in 'all others'. The engineering industry is very heterogeneous and much of it would not rank as 'high technology', so progress is slow. Table 11(b) takes the electronics industry, which might be regarded as a high–technology group, and the most advanced sub–group within it, namely computer manufacture. Comparison of the first two columns of figures shows how in 1971** movement to more advanced industry shifted the balance of employment up the scale of qualifications. Columns three and four are alternative estimates[3 & 4] of the labour requirements of the computer manufacturing industry in 1980.[†] Semi–skilled and unskilled labour has been eliminated; the ratio of technicians to craftsmen has increased from less than five to one, to nine or ten to one; and the ratio of scientists and technologists to technicians has increased from less than one in five, to better than one in two. There is then the problem of

Occupation	%in 1969/70	% in 1979/80
Managerial staff	3.4	4.9
Scientists and technologists	1.9	2.4
Technicians including draughtsmen	7.4	7.7
Administrative and professional staff	4.1	5.6
Clerical and office staff	12.3	11.1
Supervisors, including foremen	4.2	5.1
Craftsmen	19.6	18.3
Operators, with at least one week's training	34.4	35.3
All others (excluding canteen)	12.7	9.6
Total numbers employed (excluding canteen)	3,422,280	2,822,177

(a) Employment in the whole engineering industry, from EITB Annual Reports.

Table 11 (a)

Occupation	Electronics Industry	Computer Manufacturer	Computer Manufacture 1980, numbers.	
	1971, %	1971, %	(i)	(ii)
Scientists and technologists	4.75	10.55	5,000	7,500
Technicians	37	56	9,000	10,000
Other non-manual Skilled workers (craftsmen)	13	12	1,000	1,000
Semi-skilled	36	16	–	–
Unskilled	9	5	d	–

(b) Employment in the whole electronics industry and in computer manufacturing.

Table 11 (b)

the change in skills required for the move to employment in high-technology industries. This is probably behind the combination of a steady increase in unemployment with a rising national output (GDP) which has occurred since 1966, as illustrated in the graph. This phenomenon has been generally recognised — the House of Lords Committee on Unemployment referred to 'the retreat from full employment after 1966' and the Department of Employment set up a working party to investigate possible causes of the change which occurred about 1966 (see 'Why 1966 ?' in the Appendix) — but no definite explanation has been forthcoming. The change has been slow but perceptible in the past but is now speeding up. The human aspect of this problem will be considered in Chapter 6.

The trends shown in Table11 antedated the introduction of robots. With them, one can say as a rule–of–thumb that in any repetitive manufacturing process, 95% of the shop–floor work–force can be eliminated and the remaining 5% will then be occupied with supervision, fault diagnosis and rectification ('trouble shooting'), and maintenance, requiring for the most part training of technician type. Manual skills will no longer be marketable as such, though some will be included in the technician's repertoire, and semi–skilled and unskilled jobs will disappear altogether. Particular examples are (a) that the American Can Company proposed to build in Merseyside, an area in which industrial development is sought specifically in order to combat unemployment, a factory turning out 500 million cans a year which would need only five men on the factory floor[5]; and (b) that according to newspaper comments[6] on the government grants involved, a factory is to be built near Colchester which will employ only one man in its operation, though considerable numbers will be employed during construction. This reduction in shop–floor work-force is not necessarily limited to high–volume repetitive work. There is now beginning to be a vogue for FMS (Flexible Machining System) installations in which a computer–controlled machining centre can be programmed and re–programmed to perform a variety of tasks for different types of product. There has been much recent activity on FMS, but so far there are still disappointing reports on actual applications. Obviously some occupations will not be much affected: much construction work (both buildings and roads), and all forms of maintenance which must be carried out on site and are not susceptible to extreme automation. Likewise most of the pure service activities, from hairdressing to professional services like those of

• • •   GDP relative to 1954 = 100

✗   Annual average percentage umemployment.

- - - - -   Line of possible long term trend since 1966.

Figure 4

The simultaneous growth of unemployment and of GDP.

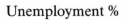

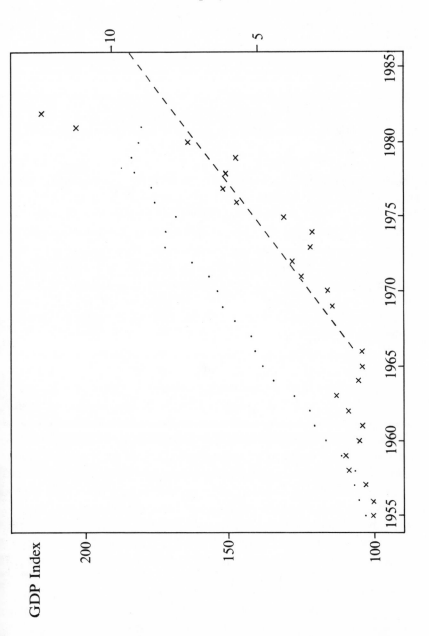

doctors, will be largely unaffected. There may be marginal effects, such as a reduction in the number of personnel managers corresponding to the reduction in employment in large units and a diminution in clerical work resulting from introduction of the 'electronic office', with computerised databases instead of files of papers.

An estimate of the number of jobs which will eventually disappear from the occupations listed in the 1971 Census[††] is shown in Table 12. Judging by past history, 'eventually' may mean over a period of 15 to 30 years, but the period may be shorter as the change speeds up. The rationale of the estimates shown in Table 12 is given in Chapter Note 1.

So much for the destruction of jobs, but one must look also at the creation of new jobs, for which hopes are usually pinned on (a) small firms and (b) firms associated with new technology. With regard to (a), one notes that over the 9 years 1971—9 inclusive the censuses of production showed that in manufacturing, the proportion of employment in enterprises employing fewer than 200 rose very slowly from 21% to 23%, but at the same time very large enterprises, with more than 20,000 employees, increased their share from 18% to 24%, probably because of amalgamations and take–overs of medium–sized enterprises. From this it does not look as though small firms have been, or are ever likely to be, 'great soakers–up of labour' as is sometimes said. The misunderstanding probably arises partly because there are so many small enterprises but also, and mainly, because the number of employees in the range of businesses with 1—99 employees is much greater than that in any other *single size range* below 15,000. Moreover, a detailed study of the flow of persons through the state of unemployment in June 1980[7] revealed that the number of unemployed coming from small firms was higher than their share of total employment would warrant. This is because small firms fail more frequently than large ones.[‡] All told, this does not confirm the hope that small firms will absorb a large part of the unemployed. Under the heading of 'Firms associated with new technology' one thinks first of the electronics industry, especially in the light of what the Prime Minister said at the IT 82 Conference, that in Scotland electronics employs more people than steel and shipbuilding. But the Director of the Electronics Division of the Scottish Development Agency has since reported that in 1983 there were 40,000 employed in the Scottish electronics industry, not that much more than the number employed

Class of occupation	Loss of jobs %	Numbers
II Miners and quarrymen	125	58,600
III Gas, coke and chemical makers	50	67,400
IV Glass and ceramics makers	25	22,200
V Furnace, forge, foundry, rolling mill workers	75	120,100
VI Electrical and electronic workers	95	73,700
029 Assemblers		
VII Engineering & allied trades workers, n.e.c.*	50	1,398,400
VIII Woodworkers	25	102,400
IX Leather workers	50	55,700
X Textile workers	75	222,300
XI Clothing workers		
076 Sewers and embroiderers	90	214,900
Rest of Class XI	25	42,400
XII Food, drink and tobacco		
079 Butchers and meat cutters	20	23,216
081 Food processors n.e.c.*	80	107,500
Rest of class XII	50	52,300
XIII Paper and printing workers	50	153,700
XIV Makers of other products	90	273,900
XV Contruction workers		
098 Construction workers n.e.c.*	95	223,700
XVI Painters and decorators	5	13,400
XVII Drivers of other than road vehicles	30	88,400
XVIII Labourers n.e.c.*	100	1,097,500
XX Warehousemen, store keepers, packers, bottlers	20	153,000
XXI Clerical workers		
139 Clerks, cashiers	70	1,694,500
Rest of class XXI	30	326,300
XXIV Administrators and managers	20	348,800
XXVII Inadequately described	50	325,600
Total number:		7,259,900

*n.e.c. = not elsewhere classified
Loss of jobs from the occupations listed in the 1971 census. Where a class or part of a class is omitted, the estimated loss is zero.

Table 12

in the 1960's.[17] However, it depends how one defines 'electronics industry'. If one takes 'Information Technology' alone one estimate[8] is of a total employment of 160,000. On the other hand, data collected by the Electronics Economic Development Committee (EDC)[9] showed that if a wider description of the electronics industry was taken, to include Components, Consumer Products like TV receivers, tape recorders and cassette players, Capital Equipment like radio transmitters and radar and Information Technology, including photocopiers and computer services, then *this* electronics industry had a decline in total employment from 565,000 in 1970 to 525,000 in 1980. On the definition used here, even Information Technology showed a declining employment, from 186,000 in 1970 to 167,000 in 1980. Neither the smallness of the IT group nor the decline in employment in a more widely defined electronics industry offers hope that electronics will do much towards absorbing three million or more unemployed. It has already been argued in Chapter 4 that automation in manufacturing industry must destroy more jobs than it creates, so that the new industry of manufacturing the robots and the like cannot provide the solution.

The general situation is well summarised in the introduction to an international survey covering UK, West Germany, France, Belgium, Italy, Norway, Denmark, Sweden and Spain.[10] The comment is 'Many people think that the problem will go away when the recession ends. Business men know better'. An earlier report from the Economist Intelligence Unit[11] also concluded that there will never again be 'full employment' in the sense of the hours per week etc. with which we are familiar. However, we need not accept uncritically the conclusion of the international survey that 'Most western countries will be forced to accept a higher level of unemployment in the future'. It may be that the greater technological complexity of industry and higher standards of welfare and of expectation of minimum wage will raise the 'full employment' level (or perhaps the NAIR level) of unemployment from the Beveridge estimate of 3% and the 1950's level of 1—2% to perhaps 5—6% (compare 5% in 1979). There is, however, no reason to accept unemployment levels of 10% and upwards.

An optimistic assumption is that the present unemployment figure of over 3 million in the UK includes

(a) the unemployment level of 1971,

(b) additional cyclical unemployment (i.e. that due to 'the recession')

(c) the first instalment of job destruction by new technology.

The total size of the long term problem is, on that basis, the sum of the 1971 unemployed, 1¼ million, and the expected loss of 1971 jobs, 7¼ million, making a total of 8½ million. Some correction is needed for size of population also: this increases the immediate problem and so in practice is included in (b). Its long–term effect is unpredictable because that depends on the timing of other changes. The important thing is not to regard this as 8½ million unemployed but as a number to be redeployed and therefore probably re–trained. If we assume 1 million continuing unemployed (roughly 4% unemployment) there are 7½ million new jobs to be found within a work–force of about 25 million; and it is a striking coincidence that recent American studies[12] have suggested the need to re–train 30 million out of a work–force of about 100 million.

The problem is complicated by the need on social and political grounds to do something quickly for the over 3 million at present unemployed, as well as preparing for the long term changes. Assuming that there can be quick enough action that the degree of penetration of automation in industry (and hence job destruction) has not changed materially in the meantime, a return to full economic activity might absorb about 1 million, a figure which is justified as follows. A peak of production was achieved in the second quarter of 1979 (seasonally adjusted) and had an index value of 115.1 relative to 1975 = 100, whereas the present value of index is near 100. Full recovery of economic activity several years later should lead to an index of at least 115—120. The majority of firms say that they could increase output by 10% without any increase in work force, so an increase in employment of about 4% is proposed for an increase in output of 15—20%. This is very far from doubling UK productivity to match that of other advanced countries,[13] but is consistent with the slow change of recent years. Then in addition there must be a continuation of the historical trends towards (a) less work (see Chapter 7 on work sharing) and (b) transfer from production to service industries. Table 10 shows that over the period 1971—1982 employment in service industries increased by nearly 1¾ million, so a further ½ million does not seem impossible. A possible treatment of the immediate problem might then be as in Table 13(a) (the arguments about choice of retiring age are reviewed in Chapter 7). The unemployment rate of 4% may seem high, but remember that it was 5% in 1979. The availability of *skilled* workers may be a difficulty for items (b) and (c); and the place of the unskilled in future employment remains a problem. In the long term it was estimated that 7¼ million of the 1971 jobs would be liable to disappear and that with 1¼ million unemployed in 1971 there would be 8½ million persons to account for. Table 13(a) suggests methods of dealing with 3¼ million quickly; and long-term arrangements for a further 5¼ million are sketched out in Table 13(b).pNote that 10% reduction in effective labour force due to reduction in hours per week is *not* the same as 10% reduction in hours per week, because productivity per hour tends to increase as hours of work decrease. The ratio of employment in production to service industries in Britain is now roughly 40:60, i.e. approaching 15 million in service industries. The long term shift of a further 1½ million to service industries (leaving ½ million for new production jobs) would then represent only 10% increase in employment in service industries, which should present no difficulty. 'Further change in working life' is deliberately left vague because some flexibility is necessary in order to meet the uncertainties of long term developments. It could mean change in number of weeks worked per year, change of retiring age or number of years devoted to education. The last could result from a change in the school leaving age, post-school vocational training or mid-life re-training. Alternatively, if the number of new jobs arising is much greater than has been assumed here, the changes suggested in Table 13(b) could be reduced.

One must also look at the *cost* of creating jobs, both the capital cost and the running cost. The capital costs are difficult to estimate though there are some figures available which suggest an average of £10,000 or more for each *traditional* job in manufacturing industry. Two examples are;

(a) a grant of £90 million to Northern Ireland was expected to produce 9,000 jobs.

(b) the total value of plant assets of UK manufacturing industry is estimated at £150 billion for a work-force of a little under 10 million. This would suggest a figure of about £15,000 per worker. This estimate of value of assets is from Table 14.21 of Annual Abstract of Statistics 1982.

(a)	Male retiring age reduced from 65 to 60 (This would include 200,000 now unemployed)	¾ million
(b)	General economic revival	1 million
(c)	New and service industries	½ million
(d)	Residual unemployed	1 million
	TOTAL	3¼ million

(a) Short-term reduction of unemployment

(a)	10% due to reduced hours per week	2½ million
(b)	Transfer to new and service industries	2 million
(c)	Further change in working life	¾ million
	TOTAL	5¼ million

(b) Possibilities for long term change in employment

Table 13

In Table 13(a), item (a) does not involve capital expenditure; and its running cost will be examined in the chapter on 'work sharing'. Return to previous employment, under item (b) of the table, should not require much capital investment, but some old equipment will have been scrapped, some moth-balled and in some cases a little additional equipment will be required to handle increased production (with higher productivity). It therefore seems wise to allow a sum of £1,000 per worker on average, which would amount to £1 billion for a million workers. This money would come in the main from retained profits and private investors hoping for a return on it from anticipated profits. Item (c) needs to be divided between new manufacturing industries and service industries. In the absence of a detailed analysis, suppose that it is split equally between them. One can suggest enormous capital sums per worker by quoting a fully automated factory which is to cost millions of pounds to build but will employ only one shop-floor worker; but it is probably more realistic for the short term to take the example of a new factory (for the production of robots by Unimation, at Telford) which is estimated to cost £10 million and provide 250 jobs. On this scale of £40,000 per job[‡‡] the capital cost of ¼ million jobs in new industries would be £10 billion, again to be found from the private sector. There are no accessible figures for investment in the service industries, but the nominal figure of £1,000 per additional worker would indicate another £250 million of which some would come from the private sector. This is asking the private sector to find over £11 billion in total. For comparison, the present total market value of UK stock exchange listed investments is over £100 billion and insurance and pension funds invested £10½ billion during 1981

Running costs for early retirement are analysed in Chapter 7. The running costs associated with (b) and part of (c) would fall on the private sector, but this would be covered as long as the employment produced an added value[§] greater than the wage cost. On the other hand, part of the service employment would be in the public sector. The amount here suggested, a quarter of a million jobs, could probably be carried within the present fiscal structure. But there has been a suggestion[14] that 500,000 more jobs could be created in education on, 250,000 in medical equipment and service and 500,000 in energy; and this is besides frequent references to the needs of elements of the physical infrastructure of the country such as sewers and housing which would also create employment. All of these would have to be paid for out of the public purse, even though the resulting employment (in the construction industry for example) would contribute to item (b) in Table 13(a). Such a massive increase in public spending, say £10 billion a year, would require either increased taxation (central and local) or a doubling of government borrowing. The latter could not be maintained indefinitely and it is an interesting question whether in the trend from production to service industries the latter will include such a proportion of community services that taxes will have to be increased. This might be jústified on the ground that the cost of manufactured goods will continue to decrease so much that even after higher taxation the real disposable income will be greater than in the past; but it must be remembered that the difference between gross pay and take-home pay is a constant cause of discontent. It is also an unfortunate experience both in the UK and in the USA that reduction in taxation does not automatically lead to an increase in productive investment. What is needed for the latter, in a free society, is the prospect of profit. This is both a necessary and a sufficient condition for investment in industry. In any case, the idea of a drastic *reduction* in taxation is unrealistic in the light of the need for movement from production to service industries, including a growing element of communal service.

For the long term plan, Table 11(b), one can only sketch general principles: numbers and rates of change must be determined as history evolves over a period of 15—30 years. There is, however, one field in which one cannot afford to be too vague. This is education, which in the past has been meant to equip a person for a working life of 40—50 years;.and on this time scale the probable changes of the next 15—30 years must not be ignored. This problem will be examined in Chapter 8. Since morale is so important in society it is desirable to set out targets for the future which are acceptable and workable. In particular, those whose jobs are destroyed should in the main be re-deployed, not unemployed. The first requirement is to recognise all the facts, including both those in this chapter and those in later chapters which examine the two problems of (a) finding mechanisms for sharing the work more equitably and (b) the extent to which the work-force can be trained for jobs which require intellectual rather than manual skills.

Notes for Chapter 5

Note 1. *The basis of prediction of job losses.*
Table 10 is based on the 1971 Census of Great Britain (Economic Activity Part II, 10% sample, Table 4). It is concerned only with job *losses* and does not take into account increases in certain occupations. It is also a long term estimate (perhaps 15—30 years ahead) assuming full penetration of automation in industry. The following is a commentary on each of the 27 classes of occupation, though classes which do not show a loss have been omitted from Table 10.

I. Agriculture in Britain is already very highly mechanised.

II. About 80% of this class consists of underground coal miners. Only a moderate degree of further automation is expected here, and a limited amount in quarrying, so the potential job loss for the whole of Class II is put at 25%. (Even Professor Thring's 'telechiric'[§§] mining, which has been given a further impulse by a recent underground disaster in Japan, would require the same number of workers, merely shifting them from the coal seam to a control room.)

III. Large-scale chemical process plant is already highly automated, so the scope for further labour reduction is set at 50%.

IV. This includes 'the manufacture of 'china and glass' for domestic use, which involves a substantial element of hand work on aesthetic and luxury grounds, so the loss for the whole of Class IV is estimated at 25%.

V. The most numerous occupation in this class is 020, the making of foundry moulds and cores, which could, in principle, be fully automated. On the other hand, there will be a few 'one off' mould-making jobs and some other jobs in Class V for which automation would not be feasible. Therefore a figure of 75% has been adopted for the whole of Class V.

VI. Occupation 029, assemblers, could be fully automated. The remainder of the Class appears to be concerned mainly with installation and maintenance, which could not be automated.

VII. Although one thinks of engineering factories as the most obvious target for 100% automation, this Class includes steel erectors, plumbers and auto engineers who will largely be engaged in 'field' work in contrast to factory work. An overall figure of 50% was therefore adopted.

VIII. Although there is a trend towards factory production of builders' joinery (doors, window frames, roof trusses) there is still a great deal of site work, and some hand work in furniture manufacture. This is regarded as a semi-service industry with probable job loss of only 25%.

IX. There is scope for automation in the mass production of footwear, (the same workers are likely to be kept on when plastic is substituted for leather) and there is a considerable demand for hand-work on aesthetic and luxury grounds. Hence an overall figure of 50%.

X. Standardised spinning, weaving and dying can be fully automated, but there will be some element of luxury trade. Therefore 75% was taken overall.

XI. Standardised sewing and embroidery can be fully automated: the figure of 90%, rather than 95%, allows a small margin for luxury work. 25% has been adopted for the remainder of the clothing industry.

XII. One cannot see a great deal of scope for automating the work of butchers and meat cutters, though some streamlining is to be expected: hence 20%. 'Food processors n.e.c.' are probably mainly concerned with manufactured foods, so their work could be largely automated: hence 80%. A figure of 50% has been adopted for the remainder of Class XII. There is a wide difference between the added value[§] per employee in different establishments, a point which has just been emphasised by a long-established Wiltshire meat firm going out of business.

XIII. One hears of the need for new technology in newspaper publishing and the same must be true of book publishing. But there is also a great deal of work undertaken by jobbing printers. An overall figure of 50% has therefore been adopted.

XIV. 'Makers of other products' is very vague. The figure of 95% assumes that full automation would be possible, and Japanese reports of the use of robots in small businesses support this view.

XV. 'Construction workers n.e.c.' are assumed to be mainly labourers and other unskilled workers, whose jobs could be largely eliminated. The remainder of Class XV would be field workers whose jobs could not be automated.

XVI. 'Painters and decorators' in the household sense are field workers who cannot readily be replaced (except by DIY and new materials). But Class XVI includes aerographers, paint sprayers and coach painters whose numbers may be reduced. The figure of 5% allows for this.

XVII. This is a very mixed class which includes drivers of stationary engines and cranes, operators of earth–moving and other construction machinery, materials–handling plant operators n.e.c. Much of this is field work, but an overall reduction of 30% might be possible.

XVIII. There will be no jobs for unskilled labourers.

XIX. Loss from the railways can be balanced by gains in road transport.

XX. Even a fully automated factory will need someone like a store keeper to check inward and outward flows. Warehouses are part of the distributive sector, but some reduction of labour can be achieved by the automatic picking of orders. Packing and bottling is already well automated. A reduction of 20% is estimated for the whole Class.

XXI. Filing clerks will be eliminated by computerised information storage and retrieval. Many cashiers will be eliminated through the trend towards 'the cashless society'. Some other clerical workers will be displaced through the introduction of word processors, the paperless office etc.

XXII. No comment.

XXIII. No comment.

XXIV. At least some personnel managers will be eliminated as a result of the reduction in the manufacturing work force.

XXV. No comment.

XXVI. No comment

XXVII. Where the occupation is inadequately described one can only take a 50/50 chance on whether it is one which will be preserved or lost.

GENERAL: More precise forecasts might be obtained by a detailed scrutiny of each industry. But as the timing is in any case very uncertain, the numbers at any given date are necessarily liable to a considerable range of variation. The list above represents an estimate only of the ultimate result when all industries have been fully penetrated by automation. None the less, it is foolish to refuse to move in the right direction because the extent and rate of movement is not precisely known. We have enough warning from the fact that the minimum unemployment even at peaks of economic activity has risen progressively since 1966.

Note 2. *The cost of creating jobs*
Some examples have come to hand recently;

(i) the Unimation Corporation has proposed spending £10 million on a new factory in Telford, England, to manufacture robots. This is expected to provide 250 jobs, so the cost is £40,000 per job.

(ii) Hyster Fork Lift Trucks in Invine, Scotland, has undertaken (in return for a reduction in present wages) to invest £40 million in a new factory which will provide 1,000 jobs, again £40,000 per job.

(iii) The DEC computer company (long known for its PDP11 computer) proposes to establish an R & D centre in Reading costing £7 million. This would have 50 staff initially and 300 eventually. This would work out at £140,000 per job initially, falling to £23,000 eventually if expansion to full numbers can be achieved without any supplementary capital expenditure.

(iv) The Commodore computer company has proposed the building of a factory in Corby, to manufacture computers. This is estimated to cost £20 million and provide 'over 300' jobs — say £60,000 per job.

One wonders whether the capital cost would be so high for an enterprise based on software. Example (iii) is analagous to a software enterprise in that the output would result from intellectual effort and most of the staff would be of technologist and technician level, with a minimum number of skilled manual workers. Software and similar enterprises[16] offer few opportunities for manual workers, particularly the semiskilled and the unskilled, so that they are not very relevant to the problem of general unemployment.

NOTES.

* Even at 5% p.a. (compound) the value of money is halved in just over 14 years.

** 1971 was the last year for which the statistics of the electronics industry were published by HMSO.

† In 1979 the computer equipment industry in USA employed 273,400 of whom only 44% were production workers.

†† 1981 Census details of occupations were not available at the time of writing.

‡ In 1980, 113,00 new small firms were started, but 115,700 were liquidated. (Survey of Small Business, *Financial Times*, 22nd June 1983).

‡‡ See Chapter Note 2 on the cost of creating jobs.

§ See Glossary

§§ See Glossary

REFERENCES

1. William H. Beveridge, *Full Employment in a Free Society*. Allen & Unwin, London. 1944.
2. Samuel Brittan, *How to end the 'Monetarist' Controversy. (2nd. edn.)* The Institute of Economic Affairs, London. 1982.
3. National Economic Development Council, *Electrohic Computers SWP, Manpower Sub-committee; Final Report*. 1980.
4. R.A. Buckingham, Education and Training in Computing. *Computer Bulletin*, June 1981, pp. 22—24.
5. S. Connon, Micromisery on Merseyside, *Computing*, 13th August 1981, p. 20.
6. Lawrence D. Hills, Food for Thought in Jobless Age (letter).*The Times*, 6th January 1983 (quoting from *Sunday Times* Business News, 11th December 1982).
7. W.W. Daniels, *The Unemployed Flow. Stage 1. Interim Report*. Policy Studies Institute, London. 1981.
8. Alan Burkitt, IT won't make a dent in the dole figures. *Computing*, 16th December 1982, p. 17.
9. National Economic Development Council, *Policy for the UK Electronics Industry*. 1982.
10. Anon., Tomorrow's Jobs. *Chief Executive*, November 1982, pp. 12—19.
11. Harry Shutt, *The Jobs Crisis*. Economist Intelligence Unit, 1980.
12. Pat Choate, *Retooling the American Work Force*. Northwest-midwest Institute, Washington. 1982.
13. Frances Williams, The Cost of Higher Productivity. *The Times*, 20th October 1982.
14. Alan Burkitt, IT's Job Creation Hangs in Question. *Computing*, 13th January 1983, p. 20.

15. Tony Durham, A glimmer of hope arises from the ruins of Consett *Computing,* 17th February 1983, p. 21.
16. Paul Walton. 1983 heralds a big move into software sales. *Computing,* 24th February 1983, pp. 14—15.
17. Ken Smith, The overview *IEE News September 1983, Supplement 'Scotland',* p. 29.
18. Anon., Estimates of employees in employment. *Employment Gazette,* December 1983, pp. 508—509.

Chapter 6

JOBS FOR PEOPLE

Should it be 'Jobs for people' or 'People for jobs'? Before the Second World War and for twenty years afterwards, the latter was probably the general view: jobs were created either by entrepreneurs or by communal need, and one looked for people to fill the jobs. Those left over after all the jobs were filled were relatively few in number and not given a great deal of consideration. (In earlier times, — though prevailing well into this century — 'work' was created in 'work houses' for those who could not find jobs or other means of maintaining themselves. The policy was to make conditions there so harsh that nobody would go there if they could avoid it.) The minimum material needs of the unemployed are now cared for by the 'welfare state' and to some extent they share in the generally rising standard of living. With registered unemployment between 1% and 2% it could be supposed that the jobless consisted of a hard core of unemployables plus a number who were unemployed between one job and another. In 1944 Beveridge[1] suggested that 3% would be the minimum unemployment practicable, including 1% of seasonal unemployment and discounting any disturbing influence from outside the UK. Beveridge referred to the unemployed as 'a reserve of labour', meaning that without this reserve it would not always be possible to find people to fill jobs and such shortage of labour could be expected to lead to inflation. In times of high unemployment, however, it is argued that the state has a duty to provide jobs and that new jobs should be brought into areas of particularly high unemployment, rather than expecting unemployed workers to uproot their homes and destroy existing communities by moving in search of employment elsewhere. In practice, of course, the prospects for the majority of finding work elsewhere in times of mass unemployment are not good enough to justify moving. This is one aspect of the idea of jobs for people. The opposite idea, people for jobs, is seen in the suggestion that a firm should set up a factory in a particular area 'because of the availability of a suitable labour force'. The whole argument is particularly relevant at a time of change in industrial structure when hopes for the reduction of unemployment are pinned (unrealistically) on the creation of new industries.

As shown in the graph in Chapter 5, unemployment has been drifting upward since 1966 while the GDP (the sum of all goods and services produced within the country) has continued a fairly steady growth. Although the recent registered unemployment of 12% is not as bad as the 22% of 1932, both of these are national averages and the figures for some localities are two or more times as high. Figures like these in no way correspond to Beveridge's specification of irreducible minimum unemployment and represent an unacceptable situation. It should be clear from Chapter 4 that the trend cannot be reversed by a general increase in output to correspond with the increased productivity and the reduction of unemployment by work sharing is explored in Chapter 7. The purpose of this chapter is to consider how far different kinds of people require different kinds of job and how they can be accommodated in a progressive industrial society.

But are there really different kinds of people within the mass? The founding fathers of the United States declared it to be self-evident that all men are born equal. What about women? Were they included or ignored? They now provide a third or more of the work-force in industrialised countries, so they must not be ignored. But what is meant by 'equal'? 'Equal in the sight of God' is a convenient way of dodging the issue by postulating a viewpoint which is difficult or impossible to define or understand. It is, however, certain that all men are not born alike: the author does not believe he could ever have run as fast as Steve Ovett and Sebastian Coe, however he had trained! Watching athletics on television, one notices the dominance of various ethnic groups in heavyweight boxing, in sprinting and in long-distance running; and within any community only a few individuals have exceptional singing voices. If physical characteristics are so specifically distributed, what about 'intelligence'? We know that in extreme cases accidental brain damage due to trouble at birth or subsequent injury, or deliberate damage in the form of a lobotomy, can cause significant change in behaviour and 'mental' attributes, as can drugs. On the other hand the brain is an extraordinarily versatile and flexible device which can compensate for some deficiencies by internal re-arrangement, especially if helped by training. Apart from gross damage no-one has been able to demonstrate a correlation between physical structure of the brain and 'intelligence'. (The alleged effect of environmental lead on the development of children's intelligence might be put under the heading of 'gross damage'). So is intelligence, as measured by IQ, an in-born (genetic) characteristic or is it dependent on environment? The answer is undoubtedly 'both', though the division of influence between the two factors is disputed (see Chapter Note 1). Fortunately the origin of IQ does not matter too much for the present purpose: it would take a generation or more to make a major change in the effect of the environment, though something can and should be done more quickly for the minority whose development is visibly impaired by an extremely adverse environment. Accordingly, we may take it as an experimental fact that IQ is a characteristic of a population which is normally* distributed with a mean value of 100 and a standard deviation of 15. The probability of any particular value of IQ can then be read from standard tables of this form of distribution.

One of the difficulties in IQ testing is to make the test result independent of cultural background, but it is claimed that this can be successfully achieved. Firstly, there is in general a correlation between the results of tests designed to measure IQ and other tests involving intelligence, such as vocational aptitude tests. But even the latter may be subject to cultural effects. It is rumoured that in aptitude tests for computer programming the standards set in India have to be different from those in Europe and USA. On an anecdotal level, a student from the Middle East said that engineering was easy for English boys because they were used to taking motor bikes to pieces. Secondly, there are a number of non-verbal tests within the battery of tests used to determine IQ, e.g. pattern recognition and extrapolation, the length of a series of digits which can be remembered either in forward or reverse order. Thirdly, but not yet well established, there may be a correlation between IQ and physically measurable factors such as reaction time and some features of encephelogram waveforms ('brain waves');[2] and if this is in fact established it will overcome the difficulty of cultural differences. It may well be asked whether IQ is of sufficient generality to be used as a measure for classifying people for different kinds of jobs. It is not a perfect measure of 'intelligence' and still less of employability; but it is a widely available and well researched measure which correlates well with intuitive ideas of 'intelligence' and with the requirements of different occupations. Most people think that there is some connection between intelligence and occupation;

and a refined version of the intuitive approach was the Barr scale.[3] This was established as the average of the opinions of 20 psychologists on the relative intellectual demands of 121 representative (and adequately defined) occupations. The result ranged from 0.00 for Hobo through 7.79 for Butcher, 13.08 for Graduate Teacher to 18.06 for Great Merchant (million dollar business, 1926 dollars) and to 20.71 for Inventive Genius (Edison type). The weakness of this scale is that it is essentially intuitive and the accuracy to two decimal places is not justified even when 20 intuitions are averaged. Taussig[4] adopted a broader classification into the following five groups, which seems more reasonable:

Professional

Semi-professional and business

Skilled labour (e.g. carpenters, barbers, policemen)

Semi-skilled to slightly skilled (e.g. teamsters, waiters)

Common labour

Some experimental evidence for a relation between IQ and occupation is given in Chapter Note 2.

An unfortunate politician once said on the radio that he thought it disgraceful that half the population had less than average intelligence! None the less this is the fact (the distribution of IQ is symmetrical about the mean) and the question is whether in future we can find a suitable place in our society for everyone. Some people question whether 'suitable place in society' is synonymous with 'employment'. But nearly everyone will find satisfaction, personal fulfilment, in purposeful activity which is making a contribution to the community and can give a feeling of being wanted. There is also the question whether employment implies a collective work-place such as a factory or an office. In opposition there is the concept of the 'electronic cottage', that there will be a return to cottage industry in the sense that most people will be able to work from home instead of travelling daily to a work-place. They can communicate with colleagues by telephone and also with the office computer and the computer database which takes the place of office files. This idea appeals particularly to women who wish to combine outside employment with family responsibilities; and in the long term, as human work is concentrated on the handling of information, leaving it to robots to perform all manual tasks, this mode of working could be feasible. Writers and artists already lead a kind of life which does not involve going out to work, but would it suit everyone? There is also the social life, contact with fellow workers or with customers, which is involved in most present forms of employment. It should be pointed out that most of those who analyse these problems are often of above average IQ and may have different values, attitudes and aims. They must therefore be cautious in endeavouring to assess what is appropriate for the majority of the population who have average and lower levels of IQ.

Mention of artists and writers calls to mind the point that in earlier times such artists, and scientists, depended for their livelihood on finding a patron, a rich man who was willing to spend some of his wealth in a way which led to no immediate financial return. Although there is still a little private benefaction in the Western world, the role of patron has largely devolved on the state. So this is a particularly small field of employment, including all 'academic' work, which is likely to have to be financed out of taxation. After all, the preservation of culture is just as much a service to the community at large as the maintenance of sewers: the trouble is that it is more difficult to assess value for money.

It has been shown that there is some correlation between intelligence and occupation, though there is a good deal of variation within any one occupation, which may be due to factors such as 'motivation', 'following in father's footsteps' or 'the opportunity presented itself'. In the recent past the percentage of unemployment was, for a time, less than would have been expected on grounds of IQ distribution. (Cf. the study of the ESN by A.M. Clarke, reported in Chapter Note 2.) To set the scene, note that on the upper side the value of IQ appropriate for a university honours degree course has usually been taken as 120; and on the lower side a value of 70 is taken as the border line of the ESN (educationally sub-normal) and 50 for the technically imbecile. One might then suppose that the group between 70 and 85 might have some difficulty in finding a place in a highly organised society, either in industry or in the service sector. But according to the normal distribution this range of IQ should account for 13.6% of the population, whereas *before 1966* the proportion of unemployable was much smaller at 1% or less: Beveridge implied at one point** that 1% were unemployable. Beveridge estimated the lowest practicable figure for unemployment, allowing for some seasonal work and for short-term unemployment between jobs, as

3%. The figure of 1% unemployable refers to the work-force and so excludes those in institutions. Beveridge referred to the other 2% of his assumed minimum of unemployment as a 'reservoir of labour', necessary to ensure the possibility of finding people for jobs whenever wanted. But from 1954 to 1966 unemployment did not exceed 2%, i.e. it was significantly less than Beveridge's supposed minimum value of 3%. Why cannot we keep it there now and in the future?

First there is the problem at the lower end of the scale of IQ.[†] One gets the impression from historical records that industry has in the past regarded the employment of the unskilled as something of a luxury: they were the first to go in hard times and have always been liable to a higher than average rate of unemployment. (Another reason for industry being more willing to part with the unskilled is that they can easily be replaced when the need arises.) In some recent years the Department of Employment has broken down the unemployed into six occupational groups (in the statistical section of the Employment Gazette) and in September 1979 43.1% of the male unemployed were 'general labourers'. One cannot make exact comparisons, because the census category may not agree precisely with the Department of Employment category of 'general labourers'; but the proportion of general labourers in the male working population is much less than 40%, in fact it is almost certainly less that 10%. (The percentage of general labourers in the unemployed had dropped to about 35 by 1982, not because the *number* of unemployed general labourers dropped but because the number of other unemployed increased more rapidly.) This occupational breakdown of the unemployed is not available for earlier years, but for census years one can obtain figures for the unemployment of general labourers who were not associated with any particular industry, as shown in Table 14 Thus at every census from 1931 onward the unemployment rate for general labourers has been substantially higher than the average. This is as far back as one can readily pursue the facts quantitatively, but there is qualitative evidence of a similar difficulty *before the industrial revolution.* There is a modern ring about the following comment[8] on conditions in 17—18th century England:

> 'King's data are probably not very accurate but they do serve to show that 'the feet of the body politic' were too large for the head and trunk by 1700. The poor had become an immense problem long before the Industrial Revolution... But the poor were no less

Year	Occupation number in census	% Unemployment General labourers	National average
1931	930	47.5	22.4*
1951	950	5.9	1.9**
1961	188	7.3	2.8**
1966	116	6.8	1.6
1971	114	11.8	5.9

* Beveridge estimate.
** 1951 and 1961 censuses do not distinguish *employees* as a group from self-employed and employers. These census figures for 'out of work' are therefore not identical with the usual figures for 'registered unemployed'.

Table 14

characterised by tiny smallholders, common–right holders, squatters, who occupied unauthorized cottages, on the manorial 'waste', catch–workers and the like, who were not independent of employment by others but who could or would take paid work only at seasonal peaks of demand or when trade was prosperous. These poor, perhaps a quarter of the population in the seventeenth century, caused most of the problems, partly because the livelihood of many of them was being diminished by reclamation or more intensive farming, or because of the threat to order of their precarious standard of living, and of their alleged turbulence and idleness.

We can be thankful that whatever can be said against the industrial revolution, the problem group no longer amounts to anything like a quarter of the population.

So much for the past, but what of the future? Part of the main drive of this book is that the requirement for the less skilled types of labour has been decreasing in recent years and will decrease still more in the future. Even the December 1981 White Paper 'A New Training Initiative: a Programme for Action' (*even* because government circles are very reluctant to take note of any major change in the country's occupational structure) states in paragraph 43 that in future there will be more employment at the level of technician and above, and less at semi–skilled and lower levels. A direct effect of technological change was reported in The Times of 23rd April 1982 under the headline 'Dispute in AUEW over automation'. The dispute was whether CNC machine tools should be operated by craftsmen who had operated the machines which were replaced by CNC, or by technicians who had prepared the programs for CNC. The union's national committee endorsed a resolution that craftsmen should operate the machines and should be given training in the new systems and in programming of the computer–control tapes. Various examples of the 'upward' drift of employment requirements and the reduction in total employment in high–technology industries were shown in Table11. There is no doubt that change has occurred, and it can be assumed that it will occur more quickly in future.

It is clear that the major problem is to find work for the unskilled (and to a less extent, for the semi–skilled and craftsmen). In the light of discussion earlier in this chapter, this will be equated broadly to finding employment for those whose IQ is not of the highest (regardless of the cause of that state). There is evidence[9] that even those with IQ below 50 can perform useful tasks, provided that the tasks are simple and repetitive and a sufficient period of learning is allowed. It is possible that agriculture may in the past (before it became mechanised) have provided some unskilled work: less would be required of a farm labourer in labour–intensive agriculture than of an agricultural worker using machines costing tens of thousands of pounds. Watching a demonstration of harvesting with a horse–drawn reaper–binder and separate threshing tackle, the author estimated that this employed 10 to 12 men, largely in the physical handling of sheaves of corn, in contrast to one man to drive a combine harvester plus one to drive a tractor and trailer in a shuttle service to take away the grain at intervals. The same argument can be applied to domestic service, particularly for women.[10] It is ironic that for many years engineers have had it on their consciences that the first stage of highly mechanised manufacture tended to replace craftsmanship by numerous repetitive operations. The classic example of this is the automobile assembly line which was studied by Walker and Guest[11] in 1952. This type of employment has often been condemned as 'inhuman' and labour for it obtained only by paying high wages. This is illustrated by a comment in 1949 from a Birmingham resident on the local automobile plant:

> 'Any b.... fool can earn £x a week on the assembly line, and anyone who does is a b.... fool.'

(The numerical value of £x would not be significant after so many years of inflation, but it was more than twice the wage of an engineering labourer.)

Recently there have been efforts to change this situation, either by changing from assembly line to group production or by replacing human labour by robots.

How has it come about that this repetitive work which would be suitable for those of limited intelligence has been undertaken, for the sake of the money, by more able men who hate it? It may be natural for an employer to take on the 'best' out of those who apply for a job, but an alternative long term view is that only those who are suited to the job will settle down as permanent and contented employees. A possible reason for the former policy being so frequently applied in practice is that the more able can work faster and make less exacting demands on work supervision. (They may, however, make more demands on management in other respects.) Therefore it may appear more profitable to employ the more able workers, even at a higher wage. The need for more supervision would be unattractive to management, apart from any question of speed of working, and the employment of lower grade labour would be uncommercial unless the wage rate could be correspondingly reduced. But this would amount to paying 'the rate for the person' instead of 'the rate for the job'. At present this is unacceptable: firstly because organised labour does not trust management to assess fairly the worth of the person and secondly because management does not want the responsibility of making such an assessment. One attempt to get round this difficulty is the use of some form of payment by results, either through piece–work or through productivity bonuses; but this is often a cause of friction in industrial relations and causes difficulty with indirect workers such as supervisors, inspectors, store–keepers and maintenance personnel, to say nothing of design and office staff. Profit–sharing is another possibility, but may be too indirect for shop–floor workers.

If commercial employment of low–grade labour is not practicable, the alternative is to reserve some of the repetitive work in a non–commercial organisation which the author has christened 'Omnemploy' by analogy with Remploy. Being non–commercial and distinctive it might be able to pay lower wages without coming into direct conflict with the 'rate for the job' principle. The differential wage rate would encourage any who were capable of doing so to get a job in the commercial world outside. Implementation of such a scheme would require the following:

(a)   some money for buildings, plant and working capital

(b)   some top management appointments to organise the enterprise

(c)   a large number of sympathetic supervisors.

As regards (a), could the Government's next large subvention to BL take the form of the purchase of surplus plant for transfer to Omnemploy? For (b), it would probably be possible to find a few suitable individuals who would dedicate themselves to the success of the enterprise. The critical factor might be (c), the need to obtain the services of a large number of supervisors who were both competent and sympathetic. They should preferably take a personal interest in the welfare of their workers (this is not to say that such an attitude is out of place in a commercial environment), but otherwise the number required would depend on the nature of the job, e.g. on the amount of damage resulting if faulty work passed through.[††] When radio receivers were built by assembling and wiring a large number of components, a ratio as high as one inspector per five operators was suggested, but the ratio can probably be improved substantially by careful design of the individual tasks. Even so, the need to obtain the services of numbers of supervisors who are both competent and sympathetic might be the crucial factor in the whole scheme of Omnemploy.

Rural and other crafts can provide useful employment on a small scale, since it has been shown[9] that people of low IQ can learn quite exacting tasks, though slowly. Again there are the two problems of firstly, the commercial aspect of speed of working and secondly, organisation and supervision of the work. The latter problem is eased in craft work because the ratio of assistants to principal is often small.

The proportion of the work-force who need special conditions of work has in the recent past been little over 1%; but with a decreasing demand for unskilled labour this could easily rise to something like 5% of the work-force, which is 1.25 million persons.

What is needed is not only a change of *industry* but also a change of *occupation*. In broad terms there must be a continuing shift from 'production' to 'service' industries, which often involves a change of occupation, and in addition there is an enforced move away from unskilled and semi-skilled work in manufacturing industries towards skilled technician work, i.e. towards mental rather than manual skills. Even here there is a cloud on the horizon. It is generally assumed that when a shop-floor worker is transferred from production to maintenance this represents an up-grading, at least in terms of mental skills and responsibility. But there is a threat to eliminate the mental skill in diagnosis by having a built-in system of detectors and logic which will indicate the precise location of any fault, while the skill in repair is minimised by the use of plug-in replacement units.

Many of the projects proposed 'to provide employment', e.g. the renewal of sewers and the reconstruction of derelict inner-city areas, suffer from the difficulty that they are *communal* projects and must therefore be financed by some form of taxation, whether it be water rates or income tax. If the overall productivity in Britain, measured as GDP per capita, were the same as that of leading industrial countries, such as Switzerland or West Germany, a given level of taxation would give the government and public authorities roughly twice as much money to spend. International comparisons show (to most people's astonishment) that the level of personal taxation in Britain is not unusually high — it only seems it because the disposable income after tax is low. The crucial factor, the rock on which the British economy is foundering, is *productivity*; and since a drastic increase in productivity can only come about through a reduction of employment in manufacturing industry, the question of redistribution of employment is vital.

The whole problem is emphasised by the announcement in May 1982 that the number of those unemployed for more than 12 months had nearly doubled during the past year and was then about one million out of the three million registered unemployed. The immediate problem is exacerbated by the present trend of age distribution in the population of Britain and of Western Europe: it has been estimated that in the Common Market about 4 million people a year are passing the age of 16 but only 2 million a year passing 65. One can only take consolation in the saying that every pair of hands that is born is accompanied by a mouth: in other words every producer is also a consumer, so that increase in the size of the work–force should result in an increase the in size of the market. Then why can we not use the same argument in relation to setting the unemployed to work? Firstly this argument is effective only if either we are not too dependent on imports or our exports are internationally competitive: otherwise an essential part of the strategy would be import control. But if this were necessary it would merely perpetuate low productivity and keep the standard of living in Britain well below that of other industrialised nations. It is also suggested that additional employment should be financed by borrowing rather than taxation. But borrowing is the counter–part of lending (or investment) and the latter constitutes deferment by the lender of the right to spend his money immediately on consumption. There can be no borrowing in a free society unless there are willing lenders. The reaction on interest rates comes through the question of what rate will make people willing to lend, and in recent years the rate of return after tax has tended to be less than the rate of inflation. (A true return of 2—3% is usually acceptable.) So 'spending one's way out of recession' is not an obviously acceptable policy.

Part of the cure for unemployment must be a reduction in the total amount of employment, as discussed in Chapter 7, coupled with a transfer from production to service industries. But future lack of work for the unskilled remains a major problem. It is said that most of the service industries are unwilling to take those of lowest ability and a possible reason for this is the likelihood of employees in a service industry coming into direct contact with customers: and a customer who has not thought about these problems may form a poor opinion of an organisation which has employees of low ability. (A small boy on holiday in Malta was sent out to get his hair cut and on return said it had been cut by 'a Maltese nit'.) In production industries there are the two problems, firstly that a worker of lower ability needs more supervision and secondly that if a standard wage must be paid for work which is below standard (in quantity or quality) the employer receives less value for money.

Even at the present level of unemployment (around 12%) there are local shortages of skilled labour, due to a lack of mobility which is found particularly in the UK (Chapter 5, p. 71). Labour is not like freely flowing water but more like honey in a comb: even if you re-shape the comb with a sharp knife there will be some spillage (unemployment). This lack of mobility of manual workers is due partly to housing problems and partly to social tradition. But at the professional level, and often at the technician level, opportunities for employment and promotion may occur at any location and the idea of moving one's home as a result of changing employment does not then seem unacceptable. Moreover, the person at this level expects an increase in salary with career progress and is likely to own a house and have the financial resources to undertake its sale and re-purchase elsewhere. On the other hand, change of employment usually involves some loss of pension rights; and in the past this had been deliberately arranged by employers to discourage employees from moving for a higher salary. Inflation has made this problem acute, at the same time that greater mobility of labour has been recognised as desirable. Strenuous efforts are now being made in Britain to counter these hindrances to mobility. Measures include removal and re-settlement allowances for workers who leave an area of high unemployment and provisions for pensions to be transferable from one employer to another. The transferability is complete with the government scheme SERPS (the State Earnings-related Pension Scheme which aims eventually to provide a pension of half the national average wage) but in private schemes it is usually limited to the transfer of an actuarial value which is not protected against inflation. The recent experience underlines the continuing lack of mobility. It is right in general terms to take jobs to people, rather than make people move to jobs, especially when a change in the structure of industry is involved, but it is impracticable to apply this principle always and to every individual. Clearly present measures to facilitate mobility are not enough, though the psychological barrier to mobility may be as important as the financial problems. It must also be recognised that in a time of widespread unemployment there would be no point in *everyone* moving.

The traditional method of generating skilled workers was by apprenticeship (often taking seven years), but this practice is declining for several reasons. The first is the pressure for higher wages and reluctance to sacrifice earnings for training. At the craft level this financial factor is evidenced by the fact that advertisers now consider that teenagers constitute an important market because they have a high level of disposable income. At the professional level, it was usual in the 1930's for university graduates in engineering to take a two-year graduate apprenticeship at a wage of about half the modest salary that was generally available for immediate employment, but a higher initial salary is now expected. The second follows from the fact that good apprenticeship schemes used to be in such demand that some firms took on more apprentices than they expected to retain in subsequent employment. They argued that they could then keep the best for themselves, while the training of the others was a service to industry at large. This would not find public favour nowadays and is only possible with a contractual commitment over the period of the apprenticeship. The raising of the school leaving age, the lowering of the age of majority, together with a change in the skill requirements, have led to very great pressure for reduction in the length of apprenticeships. (Leaving school at 16 plus a seven-year apprenticeship would come to age 23, whereas the age of majority is now 18.) On top of the high wage costs and the on-costs such as National Insurance, holiday pay and so forth, is the fact that proper apprentice training requires a great deal of effort by the employer and the low profitability of British industry makes many firms unwilling to incur all this expenditure and effort. If the low profitability of British industry is doubted, one need only point to the complaints about British pension funds investing abroad where profits are higher.

The overall statistical approach of Chapter 5 ignores three questions, of which the first two are related to the discussion of IQ distribution, (see Chapter Note 2):

(i) How many of those whose jobs will disappear can be upgraded to meet the increased demand for technicians and technologists? (These would be the 0.5 million included in (b) above, about 10% of the total.)

(ii) What employment is to be offered to those who are unable or unwilling to be up-graded? If service industries cannot absorb them all, the answer must be 'Omnemploy'.

(iii) Rapid change in industry requires the existence of a pool of available labour. How is this to be provided?

The third question is the most difficult. At the beginning of this chapter it was mentiond that Beveridge envisaged the unemployed acting as a 'reserve of labour'. In a theoretical society this would be unnecessary because there would be full mobility of labour; but in practice the situation will never meet the physicist's definition of reversibility, i.e. that the slightest change in circumstances will cause movement in one direction or the other. An entrepreneur looking for labour for a new enterprise is faced with two possibilities: either he may find unemployed or he will have to offer a higher than average wage (or salary) or fringe benefits, in order to attract labour away from existing jobs. It is because of the latter that absence of a reserve of unemployed labour is regarded as inflationary. A counter argument is that if the new industry is going to be more successful than older industries it can afford to pay higher wages than those of industries which may be obsolescent. The transfer may also provide a promotion for the individual. On the other hand, a new enterprise almost certainly appears to offer less job security than the large long-established organisation, though recent experience, e.g. in steel and in textiles, shows that this is not universally true.

A reservoir of labour constituted by 2% unemployment spread uniformly over everyone (scientists and technicians will be a significant part of industry's needs) would mean about 10 months' unemployment for *everyone* during a working life. Can this unemployed period be other than on the dole and social security? The first suggestion is that in times of low activity (slump or recession) industry should invest in long-term research and development. Firms doing so would thus maintain their own reserve of specialised labour. Industry would probably say that this was economically impracticable today, but in 1930 Metropolitan Vickers adopted this policy and amongst other things developed a series of oils and greases for use in a vacuum which revolutionised vacuum technology for many years. Research in universities offers another resort for scientists and technicians. PhD studentships can sometimes be cut short if there is a sufficiently attractive offer of employment, or the stay in the university may be prolonged by a post-doctoral fellowship. This area is known in academic circles as 'the academic penumbra' and it can act as a reservoir of scientists both for the universities and for industry. Much of the university research work is on three-year contracts so that there are also technicians whose long term future is not committed, though they may also benefit from the tradition for universities to avoid declaring redundancies.[‡] In all this university work the rate of remuneration is usually less than would be attached to an industrial post, a factor which is counter-balanced to some extent by the amenities of university life. None the less, it is mainly the financial differential that enables industry to draw people out of the universities.

Numerically the larger problem is that of those of lower academic attainment who will increasingly have to go into non-manufacturing occupations (e.g. butchering, on-site construction work) or service industries (e.g. retail distribution, painting and decorating). Large numbers of school leavers are expected to go through MSC courses from which they will emerge *trained* but not *experienced*. (See Chapter 8 for schemes of combined vocational training and practical experience.) Something other than idleness and social security is then needed for this pool of trainees available for work but for whom employment may well not materialise for a period of six to eighteen months after training. This seems to need the permanent establishment of something like Franklin Roosevelt's Public Works Administration, which sponsored projects of the most varied kind, from building airfields to compiling mathematical tables. This could parallel, in a wider sphere, the role of the 'academic penumbra' in its limited sphere. But both depend on Government money and therefore require what economists would describe as 'buoyant Government revenue'. More basically this depends on a high income per capita and comes back (as usual!) to a high level of productivity. Those in productive work have to pay for those not so employed.

Reduction of the effective size of the work-force by work sharing will be discussed in the next chapter. But this does not affect either the estimate from Chapter 5 that one-third of the present jobs will eventually disappear or the need for a pool of available labour.

Notes for Chapter 6

Note 1. *Is IQ heritable?*

It is a natural supposition that 'brain power' is related to the physical size of the brain and this is a physical characteristic which could well be genetically determined. After all, in the evolutionary theory of the origin of man a major factor is that the size of the 'brain box' progressively increases as one passes from apes through the hominoids to homo sapiens. It therefore comes as a surprise that intelligence does not seem to be diminished when a large part of the volume inside the skull, which would normally be filled with brain tissue, is filled only with fluid. But this is the finding of recent studies (particularly by Professor Lorber at the University of Sheffield) on children suffering from hydrocephalus (water on the brain). The condition can be controlled by surgically fitting a drainage tube, to bypass the natural mechanism which is for some reason inoperative, but the pressure of fluid may already have restricted the brain tissue to a comparatively thin layer just inside the skull. Such persons do not seem to suffer loss of intelligence. All that is positively known about the brain is that it consists of an unimaginably large array of nerve cells and that the way in which these react with one another may be influenced by drugs. (There is also evidence of localisation of particular functions in particular parts of the brain.) A possible hypothesis is that the pattern in which the cells are interconnected is more important than the total number of cells. A larger volume gives more scope for complex patterns of connection, but even a hundred-fold reduction in quantity, from one hundred thousand million to one thousand million cells, may not completely destroy the quality of interconnection which would otherwise be there.

How far this trait of the quality of interconnection might be inherited is a matter for conjecture, though there is statistical evidence on the inheritance of intelligence. Investigation of the latter is difficult because it is not possible to make controlled experiments on selective breeding of human beings. Evidence therefore comes primarily from the study of identical twins who have been separated at an early age and from the study of adopted children. The latter have a common environment but differing genetic origins, the opposite of the separated identical twins. There is still controversy over the relative contributions of heredity and environment but as a result of all the evidence Professor A. Jensen (Professor of Educational Psychology at the University of California, Berkeley) suggests[12] that intelligence is about 70% inherited. But this is subject to three caveats:

(i) Where there is a difference in mean value of IQ between two groups, e.g groups of different racial origins, the possible variation of IQ within each group is so large that membership of a particular group must not be taken as prima facie evidence of higher or lower intelligence.

(ii) There is a phenomenon called 'regression towards the mean' which should ensure genetically that most people have about average IQ. If one parent has IQ over 100 and the other below, then although individual offspring may have a random variation in either direction the average over a number of cases is expected to be near the mean. (This may have something to do with the Lancashire saying about the rise and fall of a family business, 'from clogs to clogs in three generations'.) This may be partially nullified by 'assortative mating' i.e. the tendency for people to choose spouses of comparable IQ. This has led to the setting up in USA of a sperm bank derived from Nobel Laureates and other eminent intellectuals, called the 'Repository for Germinal Choice.

(iii) Development may be retarded by a very adverse environment. In such cases amelioration of the environment can produce an immediate improvement in IQ; but it has been questioned how far this improvement is fundamental and enduring beyond childhood.

It has recently been found[13] that IQ in Japan had risen appreciably during the 30 years following the 1939—45 war. Critical examination of the data by Flynn[14] led to the conclusion that the average IQ in Japan had risen nearly 15 points in the 24 years from 1951 to 1975 while the average IQ in USA had risen nearly 14 points in the 42 years from 1933 to 1975, and the Japanese were nearly 7 points ahead in 1975. The shortness of time (of the order of one generation) precludes any genetic explanation of an effect which could be followed in progress during that time; and it seems unlikely that the physical environment, consisting of such factors as nutrition, housing, medical care and freedom from environmental pollution, was significantly better in Japan than in USA, though the question of nutrition is in itself controversial. It has been suggested (BBC Radio 4, The Food Programme, 13th February 1983) that the introduction of American foodstuffs has increased the stature of the Japanese but decreased their stamina. If this is so, the possible effect on intelligence is quite unpredictable. A difference in mental environment, for example in education, is a possibility but Flynn will not consider any specific causes, saying 'Our ignorance makes such speculation seem little short of bizarre.'

Note 2. *IQ and occupation.*
Besides the intuitive approach, there is some scattered experimental evidence which relates to a correlation between IQ and occupation. The largest study is of the careers of 10,000 men[5] who had been given *aptitude* tests in 1943. Note that there was no IQ test as such, but 17 different aptitude tests which were arranged in five groups. The group with the title 'General Intellectual' contained four tests, while the other group titles were 'Numerical', 'Perceptual—Spatial', 'Mechanical' and 'Psycho—Motor'. (The last explored dexterity plus brain-muscle co-ordination.) On a sample of 22 current occupations the variance of test scores between groups was found to be slightly less than half the variance within the groups. In non-statistical language this means that there was a detectable relation between scores in the aptitude tests and subsequent occupations, although there was great variability within each occupation. Among others, this must be applied to the 'General Intellectual' test.

Some relation between occupation and IQ at the lower end of the scale is indicated by the work of Baller and others who studied the occupational careers, over 29 years,[6] of some 'mildly subnormal' persons in the city of Lincoln, Nebraska. They investigated the eventual occupation in 1964 of three groups, each of 206 pupils from the 1935 school rolls. The 'low' group, with IQ about 60, had been withdrawn from the normal school curriculum; there was a 'middle' group with IQ about 80; and a 'high' group drawn from the rest of the school rolls to match the individuals in the 'low' group in terms of age, sex, background and length of school-age residence in Lincoln. Of the 'low' group, 48% were employed as unskilled labour and 23% as semi-skilled, while only 62% of the total were entirely self-supporting. It is notable that *all* the occupations in the 'high' group were 'white collar'.

The extent of employment for the low end of the IQ scale can be inferred from a study by A.M. Clarke[7] who started with the supposition that 2% of the population, corresponding to an IQ from just under 70 downward and therefore classified as educationally sub–normal, could be expected to have difficulty in finding employment. In 1966 the population of England and Wales was 48 million, so 2% of this represented 960,000 persons. But the total populations of institutions and special units, together with their waiting lists, accounted for only 253,000 persons at that time. It follows from this study that over two–thirds of the ESN were in the community at large, and were either self–supporting or cared for by their families. In terms of national figures for population and work–force, one would expect rather less than half of the balance of 707,000 to be in the work–force, say 300,000. But this is roughly the amount of *total* unemployment at that time and there must have been some short–term unemployment and unemployment for other reasons, so some of the ESN must have been in employment. This accords with the finding at Lincoln, Nebraska, that only 38% of a similar group were not entirely self–supporting. The number of 'unemployables' in England in the 1960's was probably less than the popular estimate of a quarter of a million, but it does not follow that the same is true now or will be in future if only normal commercial employment is available.

NOTES

* 'Normal' here is taken to be according to the 'normal law of errors' or Gaussian distribution. (See Glossary)

** Beveridge[1] p. 128: 'For five months June to October 1937, the unemployment rate in London was 6.0 or a little less. Of those unemployed in June, one–sixth had been unemployed for six months or more. It is not unreasonable to assume that most persons who, for more than six months, were unable to obtain any kind of employment in London, in the middle of 1937, had some personal disabilities of physique, age or character, predisposing them to unemployment.'

† This is tacitly assuming a close correlation between IQ and occupation.

†† This is assuming that one does not separate the functions of *supervision of production* and *inspection*. Separation is a guarantee of independence, but is otherwise extravagant. (See Glossary)

115

‡ It has been customary in the UK for 'tenure' to be given to all university lecturers, which means that once the three years of probation is passed a lecturer is guaranteed a job in the same university until retirement; and this is written into the charters of most universities. But the cut in Government funds to universities has led in 1983 to the sort of situation in which commercial organisations would terminate appointments because of lack of funds, such dismissals nowadays being called 'redundancies'. The Government has been pressing universities to change their charters so as to allow redundancies, a change which is naturally being resisted by university staffs. The outcome of this struggle is not known yet (up to December 1983).

References

1. Sir William H. Beveridge, *Full Employment in a Free Society.* Allen & Unwin, London, 1944. p. 128.
2. S.F. Blinkhorn and D.E. Hendrickson. Average Evoked Responses and Psychometric Intelligence. *Nature*, Vol. 295, pp. 596—597. 1982.
3. L.M. Terman, *Genetic Studies of Genius, Vol. 1* Stanford University Press, 1926. pp. 66—71.
4. F.W, Taussig, *Principles of Economics, Vol. 2* 3rd edition. Macmillan, New York, 1921. pp. 141—144.
5. R.L. Thorndike and E. Hagen, *Ten Thousand Careers*, Wiley, New York, 1959.
6. W.R. Baller, D.C. Charles and E.L. Miller. 'Mid-life attainment of the mentally retarded.' *Genetic Psychol. Monogr.*, Vol. 75 pp. 235—329, 1967.
7. A.M. Clarke, 'Problems of employment and occupation of the mentally subnormal.' University of Hull, Typescript. 1970.
8. B.A. Holderness, *Pre-Industrial England* Dent, London, p. 35—36, 1976.
9. A.D.B. Clarke and A.M. Clarke (editors), *Mental Deficiency: the Changing Outlook* Methuen, London, 1958.
10. (As reference 7)
11. C.R. Walker and R.H. Guest, *The Man on the Assembly Line* Harvard University Press, 1952.
12. A.H. Halsey and A. Jensen, discussion on BBC Radio 3, 12th May, 1982
13. R. Lynn. IQ in Japan and the United States shows a growing disparity. *Nature*, vol. 297, pp. 222—223. 1982.

14. James R. Flynn. Lynn, the Japanese, and environmentalism. Bulletin of the *British Psychological Society*, Vol. 35, pp. 409—413. 1982.

Chapter 7

WORK SHARING

It has often been said that technological progress does not cause loss of jobs; and judging by public statements, this is the view of the present British Government. If this were so, there would be no need to consider long term methods of work sharing less brutal than the present one (1983) in which 88% of the work-force have all the work and 12% have none. The 12% is, of course, a national average and great hardship arises in localities where the local rate of unemployment is twice as great or more. The converse of this optimistic view is obviously true, that failure to adopt new technology can cause destruction of an industry with consequent loss of jobs. But as shown in Chapter 5, very many jobs will ultimately be lost and few new jobs in manufacturing industry will be created by technological progress. An interesting example is that in June 1981 it was claimed that a study of West Germany showed that technological development did not cause a loss of jobs, but in August 1981 the State Secretary in the Economics Ministry forecast unemployment in West Germany rising to two million by 1985.[1] Other general studies of national and international economic prospects (see references 10 and 11 of Chapter 5) also found that unemployment would not be eliminated by a return to the status quo, by the 'end of the recession'.

Before further considering methods of work sharing, three questions must be asked.

   (i) Do people want to work?
  (ii) Is it correct that there is a more or less fixed amount of available work, which must be shared?
 (iii) If the answers to (i) and (ii) are 'yes', *how* should the work be shared?

Following our principle of 'jobs for people' (rather than people for jobs) one must first ask whether jobs have any merit other than the obvious one, which is now questioned by some people, namely that of providing a wage which serves as a mechanism for distributing the available wealth. For it is still true for most people that 'job' is equated to 'livelihood' and a better job means a better standard of living. Once basic needs have been met the latter may include 'quality of life'. For example, an advertisement for a job in a new town may mention the advantage of being free from the rush–hour commuting of a big city. Some people question whether wages should be the sole or major means of distributing wealth and the earliest alternative proposal was Social Credit. This was originally based on a totally erroneous argument, but could be based on the broad idea that the wealth of a community includes a growing communal element and that the increase in this (capital) wealth should be matched by an increase in the money base and that the mechanism of increasing the money base should be by the issue of a regular dividend or 'social credit' to every citizen. (The idea of a money base is discussed in Chapter Note 1.) The proposed mechanism of Social Credit is not acceptable to orthodox economists, but there has been much discussion of 'negative income tax' which is a device for *redistribution* of wealth from the rich to the poor in such a way as to ensure a minimum income for everyone. One of the questions which this raises is whether a guaranteed income would discourage working, as is often alleged to happen with Social Security in Britain. What may have been unique in the history of the social sciences, an actual field experiment to try to answer such a question, was the setting up of the New Jersey Graduated Work Incentive Experiment. This experiment ran from August 1968 to September 1972 at a cost of eight million dollars (funded by a US federal organisation). Details of the statistical methods and results can be found in the two–volume report on the experiment[2] but the broad picture is as follows. Guaranteed incomes were given to samples of families which included three different racial groups and there were group differences in the effect of the guaranteed income on the total number of hours worked per week by all working members of the family:

(i) White families. The total of working hours was reduced slightly and this was interpreted as a relief of stress, for example less pressure on working mothers.

(ii) Black families. There was no significant effect.

(iii) Spanish–speaking families. There was a significant reduction in the number of hours worked.

It is clear that cultural background is relevant but there are also two reasons for treating the results as a whole with caution. The first is that all the sample families were embedded in the community of New Jersey, where the 'protestant work ethic' is probably strong, and this community background would influence the attitude of the individual sample families which were scattered within it. The second is that three years may not be long enough for full acclimatisation, to arrive at the ultimate state of equilibrium with the new conditions. The experiment was terminated partly because the welfare arrangements for all poor families in New Jersey were improved to become nearer the standard offered by the experiment to sample families.

Next, consider the two types of 'drop-out' from contemporary society. Firstly there are the complete drop-outs, represented in modern times by hippies and in medieval times by hermits. Society will accept a small number of such, especially if they have some characteristic which can be respected. (The slogan of 'Make love, not war' does not command the same respect as the aura of piety of the medieval hermit.) Secondly there are the subsistence 'farmers' who reckon to grow on a small-holding nearly everything that they need for their own use and either grow some form of cash crop or have a part-time job elsewhere, to pay for things which they cannot grow. These appear to be largely independent of the industrial society but in fact are dependent on the society in which they live for much of its infrastructure e.g. roads, postal communication, news media, and for emergency support like hospital treatment. In any case, there is just not enough land in densely populated countries for everyone to take this course of action, even if they wished to do so. There would also be the problem of providing the infrastructure if *everyone* opted for rural 'self-sufficiency'. It can therefore be assumed that something like an industrial society will continue, in which there is extreme division of labour so that a person's job makes a specialised contribution to the wealth of the community and a money wage is required in order to make the corresponding claim on all varieties of communal wealth. Wage for employment (which need not be of such a condition as to deserve the epithet of 'wage slavery') is the automatic consequence of division of labour. Work sharing is then the essential method of sharing out the wealth of the community and this is why it is needed. What wage for what work, that is, in what proportions communal wealth is to be shared out between its various members, is an entirely different question. It will not be examined in this book except in so far as it may be related to productivity changes.

Does a job provide anything else besides money? In nearly every case it provides social contact, either with fellow workers or, in some service occupations, with customers. Most people do not enjoy loneliness and the importance attached to such social contact is evidenced by the institution of substitutes for it in retirement, for example 'Darby and Joan' clubs. The fortunate also find some job satisfaction. This is most obvious in any kind of creative work, from politics to engineering design and from entertaining to teaching, to name only a few examples. But there can usually be satisfaction simply in 'a job well done' provided the job is not too monotonous for the intelligence of the person concerned. Closely related to this is the feeling of contributing to a common aim, a feeling which is not as common as it should be in Britain though company loyalty is said to be strong in Japanese industry. Given the psychological importance of the job, as well as its cash value, how much of a person's life should be occupied by paid employment? The prevalence of 'moonlighting', largely by skilled workers whose regular wage is not among the lowest, and the advertisements for some jobs with 'guaranteed overtime' suggest that many persons prefer the flexible command of goods and services which comes from more money, rather than additional leisure. This view is supported by a referendum in Switzerland on 5th December 1976, when a large majority out of a turn-out of 41.3% voted against a reduction of the standard working week from 45 to 40 hours. Commentators said that one reason was trade union fear that a reduction in working hours might lead to a reduction in earnings. (But see p. 128 .) A statutory length of working week has in the past been rare, but one can trace the customary length. Before the industrial revolution it must have been practically the hours of daylight for six days per week, except for public holidays such as saints days. The first limit imposed after the industrial revolution was 10 hours per *day*, but by the beginning of the twentieth century the customary hours in Britain were 52 per week. On welfare grounds women and young persons were then limited to shorter hours per week and excluded from night work. Further developments will therefore be considered only in terms of the hours of the adult male worker. Despite propaganda and statutory requirements for sex equality in matters other than working hours and retiring age, which at the time of writing are still separated, the author believes that most women will want to divert some of their effort to family matters and that at present women *cannot* play the same part in industrial society as men do. This situation may be modified in time, if it becomes customary for men to take on more of the household chores and care of children, but surely the biological facts preclude complete equality. It is difficult to trace working hours in Britain over a long period because of differences in the bases of statistics published at different times. In October 1938 full-time male employees over the age of 21 in *all* industries worked an average of 47.7 hours per week. In April 1950 the figure for *manufacturing* industries was 46.9 and in spite of a previous introduction of a nominal 40-hour week the hours actually worked were still 45.5 in 1970. The hours actually worked fell only with the recent recession and in October 1981 were down to 42. A longer consistent record is available for the USA by combining a summary of statistics from Colonial times to 1970,[4] with current annual publications.[5] The latest statistics refer to production workers in manufacturing industry. They started at a point similar to that in Britain, 51 hours per week in 1909, the figure then fell to 42.1 in 1930 and has been in the 39—41 range from 1950 to 1980 while the British figure was in the 45—47 range. The nominal 40-hour week in Britain is based on trade union—employer agreements, but in the USA the Fair Labor Standards Act of 1938 imposes the legal requirement that hours beyond 40 per week shall be paid at one-and-a-half times the basic rate. The difference in hours worked may also reflect a difference in the size of disposable income which can be devoted to leisure pursuits. The latter is certainly a factor in the demand for longer holidays. Furthermore 'holidays at home' are now discounted and 'cannot afford a holiday' (away from home) is regarded as an indication of financial stringency. Whatever the individual motivation may be, the delay in reducing working hours in Britain (including moonlighting) suggests that the answer to our first question, 'Do people want to work?', must be 'yes'.

The second question, whether the amount of work is limited, is more difficult. One often meets the argument that the unemployed should be paid to do something useful, such as replacing our rusting water mains, re-building worn out sewers, repairing derelict houses or clearing derelict land in our cities. The trouble is that all this communal work on the infrastructure would have to be paid for out of communal funds, i.e. out of rates and taxes. It is an interesting question whether the continuation of the historical trend in the movement of employment from production industries to service industries, some of which are concerned with communal service, will *in any case* require an increase in taxation in one form or another. The hope of escaping this is that if the country were sufficiently prosperous the *yield* from a *constant level* of taxation would increase. The objection to increasing the level of taxation (apart from its unpopularity) is that it withdraws money from private-enterprise activities. Whether or not the latter are usually more efficient than communal enterprises, the spending of money obtained by taxation is not a net gain to the economy. To take a homely example, suppose you considered employing an unemployed man to dig your garden. You would first consider whether you wanted to spend so much money. (This corresponds to the ballot-box resistance to higher taxation.) If you decided to offer the employment, you would then have to decide what other goods or services you would *do without* in order to find the wage: the worker is richer but you are poorer. Various secondary arguments come into play. If the gardener has a fairly low wage, but you are rich, it may be argued that he will spend his wage on immediate necessities but you may spend some of your money abroad or invest it in a way which does not help the economy. On the other hand, experience suggests that too much of the wage will be spent on imported goods — from French apples to Italian washing machines. But these arguments are secondary to the point that taxation represents a transfer of purchasing power from some people to others and the spending of 'Government money' can never be pure gain. It is not the amount of *work* which is limited but the amount of real *wealth*: and if employment implies wages which give a claim to goods and services, then employment is fundamentally limited by the availability of goods and services. What is needed first and foremost is higher productivity.

Thus, having concluded that everyone wants to work and that the total amount of employment is in practice limited by the amount of goods and services which are freely available to exchange for wages, the question is how the work should be shared.

A very special form of work sharing is the job-sharing scheme which has been introduced by L.P. Grice at GEC Telecommunications, a scheme which is mainly aimed at school leavers and has the additional merit that it can be implemented immediately. The arrangement is to employ two people alternately (for alternate half weeks) in place of one full-time employee. On the employees' side this means receiving only half a wage, but even this is more than a young person's (under 18) unemployment benefit, it provides training and employment which lasts longer than the MSC 'work experience' placings, and it improves the chance of the individual later obtaining a full-time job with the firm, a job for which the person is already trained. On the employer's side the cash cost in wages of two half-time employees is the same as that of one full-time employee, though the overheads may be slightly greater, but there is one significant advantage: a condition of the scheme is that each member of a pair must be prepared to work full-time in the event of unavoidable absence of the other one. This provision of automatic cover by someone who is currently familiar with the job is clearly advantageous to the employer. The trade unions appear willing, at present, to acquiesce in the scheme, since the standard rate-per-hour is paid.

This job-sharing scheme for juniors is particularly relevant to the present demographic situation, in which the excess of young people entering the employment market over older people retiring is a significant part of the social problem of unemployment. But although the scheme is praiseworthy for helping to alleviate the current problem of unemployed school leavers, it is a method of work sharing which is fundamentally inapplicable to the wider problem of the unemployed, including adults because it offers to the employee only half a normal wage, which would not be acceptable to adult workers as a permanent arrangement, though some are now temporarily on short time. From the employer's side it helps by halving the wage cost per person in training, but it would be unusual for the employer to expect so large an expansion of business that his intake of full-time employees could be doubled in a couple of years' time. If not, he will have the task of selection, which may be advantageous but disagreeable. The most favourable result would be to replace 'full-time or the dole' by 'full-time or half-time' which is still not an equitable arrangement.

A particular form of work sharing by short-time working has been proposed for school teachers in New Zealand under the title of 'four-in-five programme'.[3] The problem here is that by 1992 the number of pupils in primary schools will have fallen by 72,000 and in secondary schools by 34,000. The programme is that teachers should receive only four-fifths of salary and in return should teach for only four years out of five, the fifth year being paid leave. The scheme is said to have been tried successfully in some Canadian schools; but in common with all schemes involving short-time working, it results in a reduction of income.

Generalised work sharing requires a reduction in the effective size of work-force without reducing the number of persons in it; and there are three methods of effecting this:

(i) Reduced hours per week.
(ii) Reduced weeks per year (longer holidays).
(iii) Reduced working years per lifetime (earlier retirement and/or later commencement of employment).*

A reduction in the total number of hours in the working life is inevitable on the ground of job loss through technological progress. Choice of method should be governed by tactical considerations (the reactions of industry and of trade unions) and by psychological considerations (the use of free time and the non-financial aspects of employment).

It is clear from the historical record outlined above.that there is nothing sacrosanct about any particular number of hours per week. It would appear *prima facie* that a long term reduction of the effective size of the British labour force by one third could be achieved by reducing the number of hours actually worked per week from 45 to 30. This is based on the 8½ million surplus (out of about 25 million) which might be deduced from the 1971 Census list of occupations; and it is more than would be required because it takes no account of the creation of new jobs, particularly in service industries. So we can dismiss some of the more extravagant suggestions about future working hours.

But the practical need is for the problem of unemployment to be tackled in two parts. We have first to deal with three and a quarter million unemployed, a number which has in fact been accumulating since 1966, and then to face the long term problem set out in Chapter 5.

The trouble with relying on working hours per week is that in Britain the introduction of a nominal 40-hour week (by union-employer agreements) has made little difference to the number of hours actually worked: in fact it has been said that labour has wanted a reduction in the standard hours so that more hours could be paid at overtime rates. Overtime should be a device for dealing with exceptional urgency of production. From a management point of view it is to be discouraged because it involves a higher wage rate per hour and because of fear that working pace may slacken during normal hours in order to increase the requirement for overtime. On the other hand the engagement of additional employees (always assuming that they are available and that rate of production is not limited by capacity of plant rather than size of labour force) incurs the on-costs of National Insurance and of various welfare benefits (often reckoned to add a total of 30% to the wage bill), together with possible need for training, and risks the unpleasantness and difficulty of dismissing them if work later slackens. Overtime may therefore even be attractive to management and they will not hire additional full-time employees until the extra work load looks like being permanent.

There are two further difficulties of principle in relying on reduction of weekly hours to increase numbers employed. The first is that production per hour tends to increase when hours are shortened (in 1974 the three-day week in Britain produced some extraordinary examples of how much could be done in a limited time) so that a reduction in working hours would not necessarily cause a corresponding increase in numbers employed for the same output. In some industries there could be a counter-effect due to a constant setting-up time, so that average production per hour would be *reduced* by shortening hours per day; but this would be negligible if the reduction in hours per week were concentrated in one day. This could eventually lead to working the morning only on Friday, just as Saturday morning work preceded the five-day week. An indication of an existing tendency to lengthen the weekend is provided by railway policy, since railways offer fare concessions outside the busy periods. On this evidence, British Rail regards Friday afternoon as a busy period for inter-city trains out of Kings Cross, which are much used by people leaving London for the weekend. On French railways it appears that the busy period generally ends at 3 p.m. on Friday and after the weekend does not re-commence until 12 p.m. on Monday (apart from public holidays). The second difficulty in principle is that if the reduction in working hours were accompanied by an equal reduction in hours of plant utilisation, this would increase the capital cost of production as well as the possibility of incurring an increased labour cost for shorter working hours. (There is always pressure against any reductions in earnings per week to match the reduction in hours per week.) A reduction of the working week from 40 to 35 hours would represent a 12½% reduction in the utilisation of capital equipment in single-shift working. But nearly 80% of the GDP goes into consumption, mainly via wages and salaries,** so it seems that the capital costs must usually be small. The tendency in manufacturing industry is towards more capital-intensive operation; but the most modern automatic plant will be operated for 24 hours per day with a minimum number of personnel possibly concentrated in a single shift of 8 out of the 24 hours. The figure of 80% also includes the service industries, which in general are labour intensive and therefore not very vulnerable to capital costs. Between these two factors, the development of automatic machinery which can run virtually unmanned for some shifts of the day and the transfer of labour to service industries which are not capital–intensive, the shortening of the working week will not have much effect on overall capital costs. It is in any case manufacturing industry which is most concerned in establishing the length of working week. One might swing the factor of capital utilisation the other way, if factories which were not previously fully automated changed from a single shift of eight hours to double–day–shift working, with fewer hours in each shift. This would avoid all–night working, but would require detailed evaluation and negotiation in each enterprise. Some of the questions which would require discussion are:

How much would the saving from greater use of capital equipment allow the wage per hour to be increased?

What combination of working hours and wage rate would be acceptable to the work–force?

How much additional production could the market absorb?

What would be the effect on output and on total number employed?

In France in 1981 President Mitterand decided to implement a gradual reduction in the length of the working week, by union–employer agreement if possible, but by statute if necessary. The original proposal was to reduce the standard working week from 40 to 35 hours by stages, making a reduction of one hour in 1982 and one hour in each of the four following years. The objective was to reach a figure of 35 for the normal number of hours per week *actually worked* and the period allowed for the negotiation of the first stage was June to December 1981. A major difficulty in negotiations was union insistence that the reduction in length of the working week should not cause any reduction in weekly earnings. So in February 1982 the Labour Ministry had on its hands 650 disputes over weekly earnings, resulting from the change from 40 to 39 hours. Additionally, the CGT (Confederation Generale du Travail) refused to co–operate on the grounds that the reduction of one hour per week was insufficient to make any impact on current unemployment and the first cut should have been to 38 hours. The legislation for a 39-hour week which came into force in January 1982 also provided for a fifth week of paid holiday and for the control of overtime so that the hours actually worked should not consistently exceed the nominal 39 per week. Up to 130 hours of overtime per year (this would average 2¾ per working week) are at the free disposal of management but more than that requires authorisation. In any case, not more than 48 hours total (i.e. 9 hours of overtime) may be worked in any one week. There is also provision for calculating the effective hours per week when the actual hours are variable, e.g. when working a rotating-shift system. The French Prime Minister claimed that this would create 200,000 jobs; but an independent employers' organisation claimed that 500,000 jobs could be created in six months by transferring certain taxes from the payroll to VAT (reported in Le Monde). According to the original plan, a further reduction to 38 hours per week in 1983 should have been negotiated during 1982. But in June 1982 the franc was devalued by 5.75%, followed by a freeze on wages and prices until October and it was decided that the 39-hour week should remain in force for 1983.

Apart from argument about what has actually happened, there are four objections to regarding this French plan as generally suitable for dealing with present and future unemployment.

(a) A reduction of one hour per week in each of five successive years is too slow. It *might* keep pace with the growth of technological unemployment, but would not clear the present accumulation of unemployed.

(b) It does not create clear-cut job vacancies. An employer faced with a reduction of the working week from 40 to 39 hours, probably accompanied by a demand for an unchanged weekly wage, will endeavour to obtain the same output from the existing labour force, rather than increase the number of employees by 2½%. (Consider British Rail's variable-rostering proposals and the British Leyland tea-break dispute, both of which arose from, or were coupled with, the idea of higher productivity in return for a 39-hour week.)

(c) It does not take account of the structural factor, the need to move from old to new industries and from manufacturing to service industries.

(d)   The administration of a statutory length of working week is complicated, including, as it does, a need for provision for averaging in the case of variable hours (rotating shifts, flexitime) and for the control of overtime.

Method (ii) of work sharing — longer holidays — is included in the current French legislation, which provides for five weeks' paid holiday of which not more than four weeks may be taken at one time.

It was remarked in Chapter 1 that Switzerland is exceptional in the combination of a longer working week than average and low unemployment. Now in 1983 it is the only country in which trade unions have concluded an agreement under which a shorter working week will be accompanied by a reduction in wages. Since 1976 the working week has come down successively from 45 hours to 43 hours and 42 hours. Now it is to be reduced to 41 hours in 1986 and 40 hours in 1988; and each of these two reductions will be accompanied by a 1.2% cut in pay.[11] Since the reduction in working hours is 2.4% in the first step, this means that the cost is split equally between employer and employee. A major consideration in reaching this agreement was the preservation of the Peace Agreement between unions and employers (no strike or lock-out) which has been in force since 1937.

One of the methods proposed in this book for dealing with the current British crisis is part of method (iii), namely reduction of the male retiring age from 65 to 60. There are three objections to this:

(a)   the cost of pensions;
(b)   the loss to industry of the departure of skilled employees;
(c)   the problem of finding occupations for people during a longer life of retirement.

The 'social cost' of mass unemployment is so high that it is not right to make a decision merely on financial comparison of the cost of earlier retirement versus the cost of payments to the unemployed. Some discussion of costs is given in Chapter Note 2, but the general conclusion is that the immediate cost would in practice be less than the official estimate and could be met if the reduction of unemployment were considered sufficiently important. (There would also be long term repercussions on the finance of pension schemes of all kinds.) Comparisons have been drawn between the cost of lowering the pension age and the cost of re-possessing the Falkland Islands. This is unfair because firstly the cost of earlier retirement is an annual expense whereas the Falklands affair is (we hope) a once-only event, though there is the continuing cost of 'fortress Falklands'; and secondly because 12% unemployment means that 88% are employed and unfortunately this majority is not likely to regard elimination of unemployment with the same urgency as re-possession of the Falklands.

The issue of the loss of skilled employees is a red herring. Apart from asking how the Civil Service manages with a retiring age of 60, one can point to trends elsewhere. The Government's Job Release scheme offers some incentive to men over 62 to retire, many employees in various enterprises are being invited/urged/compelled to take 'early retirement' and it is often said that unemployed aged 60 and over have a negligible chance of re-employment. There are two other factors to consider. The first is that the pyramidal structure of industry means that key employees are likely to be a minority. According to the 1971 Census report, the number of men in the age group 65 to 69 who remained economically active was 28% of the number in the age group 60 to 64; and there is no reason why a similar result should not follow a retiring age of 60 instead of 65, thus providing more than enough to fill key positions. The inhibition of continued working resides in the contract of employment more than in the eligibility for a state pension, and there is nothing to prevent an employer from offering employment beyond the statutory pension age to employees whose services they especially value. (Some occupational pension schemes do provide for this, and the state pension is increased by about 7½% per year of deferment.) The second is that it is one of the duties of management to secure the succession to all jobs, including their own. Taking five years off the time available to do this is not going to alter the situation drastically. Another argument in favour of reducing the male retiring age is that the retirement of an employee leaves a specific vacancy which an employer would normally have expected to fill by appointing someone else. This is stated as 'normally' and in the past because the employer may nowadays consider reducing his total labour force: this is the tendency cited in the discussion of (b) above, but the elimination of a specific job requires a more thorough-going reorganisation than need be implied by a small increase in productivity. Moreover the demographic situation at present is that the age group entering employment (in Britain and in the Common Market) is larger than the age group leaving employment and in Great Britain the two will not come near equality again until after 1990.[6] This logically suggests an increase in the rate of retiring. The remaining question, of occupation for the retired, will be dealt with in the next chapter.

There has recently been a suggestion from government sources of equalising the male and female retiring ages at 63. This is a nice gesture to 'equal opportunity' but since this move is ostensibly designed to cost very little in pensions, it follows that it would have little effect on (un)employment. Since the work-force is roughly three-fifths male, the proposed change could reduce it by $2 \times 0.6 = 1.2$ man-years while increasing it by $3 \times 0.4 = 1.2$ woman-years. But there are complications. Firstly, some women workers, especially married women, have not paid enough in NHI stamps to be entitled to a pension on their own account. They would then get a pension *earlier* on the earlier retirement of their husbands. Secondly there must be some doubts, especially in the earlier years of such a scheme, about how many women would in fact work for the extra three years. This could give the scheme a more favourable effect on the employment market than the no-change attitude suggests. But in the interests of acceptability to women and predictable reduction of the work-force, the author still prefers reducing the male age to 60, in spite of higher pension costs. (See Chapter Note 2 on pension costs.)

One might seek International comparisons of retirement age, but such comparisons are inconslusive. In the USA there is said to be a tendency to extend the working life to 70 as is common in the higher ranks in the UK (e.g. judges and company directors). In Japan retirement at 55 is said to be common, though the age for state pension is 60 and the paucity of occupational pension provision results in many taking temporary employment after retiring from 'life-time' employment. An argument for later retirement is the increasing standard of health and expectation of life, while an argument for earlier retirement is the possibility of retiring young enough to *enjoy* retirement and to give more time to some activity which has previously had to be secondary to the task of earning a living. Probably the best compromise is flexibility in the age of retiring coupled with a reduction in the minimum age of entitlement to a pension.

In all this discussion of 'work sharing' there has been little mention of one of the main themes of this of this book, namely that in the long term future there will be no work for the unskilled. One is tempted to suppose that they might be included in the suggested one million unemployed (about 4% rate of unemployment), particularly as this figure is well within the range of uncertainty about future developments. But there are at present too many for that and minimisation of the number of unemployed, including the unskilled, requires the improvement of education and vocational training, as will be discussed in the next chapter. In the last resort it may be necessary to set up a special organisation, provisionally called 'Omnemploy', to cater for the very last group who cannot find normal employment.

Notes for Chapter 7

Note 1.*The money base*
The function of money is apparent from its definition as 'a tally of value, giving its possessor a claim on goods and services'. By-passing the question of how appropriate values are attached to the various goods and services, one thinks first of money in the form of cash, i.e. notes and coin issued by a government or other trusted authority. (Notes issued by private banks are sometimes in circulation.) An important feature is that money *circulates* and that therefore there need not be a total amount of money equal to the total value of goods and services in the market. So much is now paid for by cheque or credit card that the significant measure of money in circulation is not cash but 'M1', which consists of cash plus bank or similar deposits which can be drawn upon without notice (e.g. a current account with a bank or deposits in a savings bank). The ratio of total goods and services available annually (GNP) to stock of money of a particular kind is known as the *velocity* (of circulation) of that kind of money; and velocities have varied over time and differ in different countries. A high value of velocity is prima facie evidence of an efficient financial system in which the money is rapidly passed from transaction to transaction. The British Government sets great store by another measure of money called 'M3', which is the sum of M1 and time deposits. In colloquial terms, M1 is spending money but M3 is spending money plus short-term savings.

From this it is clear that while one would expect some general proportion between 'amount of money in circulation' and 'amount of goods and services in the market', the variability of the velocity means that there is no exact and constant relationship, let alone the one-to-one relationship which would justify some form of 'social credit' payment to all in cash. In Britain[8] the velocity of M1 was 7.01 in the last quarter of 1975 and 8.07 in the last quarter of 1980. In USA[9] it was 3.5 in 1960 and 6.14 in 1979. In Japan[10] it was 3.3 in 1970 and 2.9 in 1978. The velocity of M3 is even more varied: from about 3¼ in Britain through 1½ in the USA to ¾ in Japan. This is probably an indication of the propensities of the people in the various countries to leave their savings on deposit, rather than invest them directly in such things as National Savings Certificates, local authority loans, gilts or equities. It has little to do with the money base needed as a means of exchange, and rationally the propensity to leave money on deposit should vary inversely with the inflation rate. In Japan a further factor may be the scarcity of pension funds which in Britain play a major part in transforming private savings into long term investment, thereby tending to reduce M3.

On the other hand it is plausible to suggest that *capital* works should be financed by borrowing, as is considered legitimate in commercial undertakings. But the physical assets represented by the capital are subject to depreciation, which should be made good out of revenue; and it is said[7] that depreciation of community capital in Britain (e.g. sewers, housing) is not at present being made good. On the ground of increasing capital assets there would then be justification for the apparent tendency of the National Debt always to increase,[†] though in real terms it has not always increased. Much of the apparent increase is due to inflation; and by expressing national debt as a percentage of GDP, both being in current prices, one eliminates the effect of inflation and at the same time takes the reasonable viewpoint that the debt should be related to the scale of economic activity which (a) has to pay the interest on it and (b) receives benefit from it in so far as the debt may be related to capital expenditure. During the 1939—45 war the ratio of debt:GDP in UK and debt:GNP in USA rose to over 100% but it has since fallen below 60%. This includes local government debt as well as central government debt. Details for UK and USA are published in 'Financial Statistics'[8] (in February issues only) and in 'Statistical Abstract of the United States'[5] respectively.

Borrowing, however, entails lending which in turn entails deferment of consumption, i.e. resources are diverted from consumption to the capital work. The alternative to borrowing, whether it is called 'creation of credit', 'printing money' or 'government spending' is prima facie inflationary because it proposes to allow capital work to be paid for *without* deferment of consumption. A counter argument is that in some circumstances the additional money would bring into play additional resources and so not be so obviously inflationary. A full debate about inflation/deflation would be outside the scope of this book, particularly as such a debate is usually concerned with party-political attitudes.

Note 2. *The cost of reducing the male retiring age to 60.*
The cost of earlier retirement involves two factors:

(i) There is the cost to the government of retirement pensions for more people immediately, less a smaller saving on payment to the unemployed. Calculation of this requires a great deal of expertise and detailed work, to take into account the change in requirements for supplementary benefit, tax revenue which would be lost, and so on. Government sources have quoted figures between £1.5 billion (1981) and £3.6 billion (1982) but the latter is presumably for 100% retirement at the lower age. Scaling down the £3.6 billion for 60% retirement leads to £2.16 billion, without adjustment for the tax revenue from continued earnings, so £2 bllion p.a. for the first few years is a possible upper estimate. It would increase later, owing to an increasing tendency to retire at 60, but judging by past experience it would never reach the full cost.

(ii) From the point of view of a funded scheme, e.g. almost all occupational pensions, the initial deficiency due to the sudden increase in the number of pensioners will be followed by a long-term need for a higher rate of contribution;
(a) because the total contribution is less (over the shorter working life),
(b) because the time of accumulation in the fund is less and
(c) because the life expectancy is greater.
If salary and contributions increase with age the estimation of (a) and (b) is complicated. But if the contribution rate remained constant over 47 years (age 18 to 65) or 42 years (18 to 60) and interest were earned at 3% over inflation, the ratio of the two cases would be 1.22. As regards (c), according to life tables for,England and Wales (Registrar General, Mortality Statistics 1979, Series DH1 No. 8, Table 23) the male expectation of life is 12.6 years at age 65 and 16.0 at age 60. Slightly higher figures for both ages are given in a table for annuitants, due to the Institute of Actuaries and the Faculty of Actuaries, but the ratio is practically the same at 1.26. Combining the two ratios, the increase in the rate of contribution required if it is uniform throughout working life is 1.55 times. Allowing for actuarial refinements it seems wise to say

that the contribution would have to be increased by between 1.5 and 1.75 times. For a typical employee contribution at present of 6% this would mean an increase to between 9% and 10.5% of salary. It may be, however, that this is an over–estimate, because it does not allow for the benefit to the fund of the high contributions in later years when salary tends to increase with age or length of service, although the present contribution rates are based on the pension being related to *final* salary in nearly every case.

The position of the State retirement pension is not clear, apart from the fact that it is not funded, i.e. the current contributions of others, rather than the past contributions of the pensioners, go towards current pensions. But the employee's NHI contribution or 'stamp' goes towards (a) health service, (b) unemployment insurance and (c) retirement pension, the financing of each of which is split three ways between employee, employer and taxpayer. (The self–employed do not get unemployment insurance and in principle pay both employee's and employer's contribution to the others.) The same is true of the State Earnings–related Pension Scheme (SERPS) which was introduced in 1978 to ensure that by 1998 everyone would have a retirement income brought up to half the national average wage. As far as one can see none of the nine components (three benefits times three sources of finance) is firmly based on actuarial principles. Any revision of the NHI contributions to take account of earlier male retirement is therefore likely to be based on political rather than actuarial considerations. Perhaps it would be a good idea to publicise the basis of the present arrangements.

The essential point is that job sharing means wage sharing and in the context of pensions this means that those at work must support the retired, since those at work produce the whole of the goods and services for which the money is only a token. The hopeful assumption is that improved productivity, in manufacturing industry particularly, will allow the same, or more, material wealth to be produced by fewer man–hours, so that a reduction in hours of work need not lead to a reduction in material standard of living.

NOTES

* Later commencement is meant to be less clear-cut than raising the school leaving age. It might alternatively mean an increase in either full- or part-time education or vocational training such as is at present usual in Britain at both technician and craft levels and is to be available to all 16-year old school leavers.

** The technical term is 'compensation of employees'

† The apparent increase of the National Debt in money terms includes a large element of inflation. It is not easy to remove this, since any single index, such as the RPI (retail price index) would not be appropriate.

References

1. *Financial Times*, 22nd August 1981, p. 24.
2. David Kershaw and Jerilyn Fair, *The New Jersey Income-maintenance Experiment: Volume I* Academic Press, New York. 1976.
3. Lindsay Hayes, Falling rolls bring forward notion of job-sharing. *Times Educational Supplement*, 4th February 1983, p. 17.
4. *The Statistical History of the United States from Colonial Times to 1970* Basic Books Inc., New York. 1976.
5. US Bureau of the Census, *Statistical Abstract of the United States* Washington DC. Annual editions.
6. Department of Employment, The Labour Force Outlook to 1986, *Employment Gazette* April 1981, Vol. 89 No. 4, pp 167—173.
7. Crumbling Britain. *The Times* 31st August and 1st, 2nd September 1981.
8. Central Statistical Office, *Financial Statistics* HMSO monthly.
9. As reference 5.
10. *Economic Statistics Annual* Bank of Japan, Tokyo. Annually.
11. Swiss Unions agree to take cut in pay. *The Times* 11th July 1983.

Chapter 8

EDUCATION FOR LIFE

The title of this chapter is deliberately ambiguous: it means both that education should be a preparation for life and that it should be a process which continues throughout life. The educationist has to tread a tightrope between 'education for living' and 'education for employment', otherwise described as between general or liberal education and vocational education. The distinction can alternatively be made by referring to vocational *training*. In general vocational training is distinguished as a post–school activity (not post–education, because education in some form should continue throughout life) but there is inevitably a vocational element in general education. Examples in arithmetic were at one time based on men mowing meadows and hens laying eggs: perhaps they should now be based on robot productivity or length of print–out paper from a computer. (The author was once shown a computer producing print–out at such a rate that it was measured in kilometres per hour, of which every centimetre had to be read — because it consisted of pay–slips for all the employees and pensioners of French Railways. One wonders whether the mass of print–out from every large computer is read so carefully.) Moreover there are some who maintain that, whatever the content of the curriculum, the educational *system* in Britain is oriented towards the needs of employers in the existing social order. One's attitude to this depends on whether one believes in revolution or evolution. Those who believe in revolution argue that anything which helps to maintain the existence of the present social order is bad, and that even a period of anarchy would be preferable until a new social order could be established. (Anarchy is not a stable social condition and sooner or later some person or group will acquire sufficient power to impose a new social order.) If, on the other hand, one believes in evolution one has the difficult task of inculcating the social, as well as intellectual, skills which will enable the individual to find a place in existing society, but without destroying the individual's initiative which may be used to *change* society. This applies at all levels, though British universities in particular have been accused of destroying the initiative of their students. Individual university faculties can defend themselves according to circumstances — one can point to project work in engineering and a year spent abroad in modern–language courses — but the character of a 'bookworm' in the pejorative sense (i.e. concentrating entirely on a narrow range of book–learning), is probably established before entering a university. One possible cause is a desire to pass examinations which exceeds the individual's ability to do so and it is interesting that the Chinese Government has issued a warning to parents against pushing their children too hard to pass examinations for university entrance, pointing out that other (non-graduate) careers are also useful. Another possible cause of concentration on narrow book–learning is reluctance to make contact with the real world, perhaps due to lack of self–confidence.

The educational process must be examined by stages. Before entering on formal schooling every human being must first pass through the stage of infancy. Certain physical skills, such as speech and visual/muscular co–ordination, have to be established at an early age. There is no doubt also that psychological influences and development during the pre–school years are very important. The author is not qualified to comment on them in detail but the factors are mainly emotional and concerned with relationships with other people: they include such factors as affection, respect and obedience. This period is obviously very significant as is illustrated by the saying 'Give me the child to the age of three and I will have the man'. The atmosphere of home or nursery school is therefore important and the most controversial factor is that of obedience, more commonly discussed in terms of its counterpart, discipline. (Discipline may be defined as the *enforcement* of a set of rules within which the individual can operate without penalty and obedience as the *acceptance* of the rules.)

Between the ages of four and six both physical and mental skills can be developed, but to an extent which probably depends on individual ability and certainly depends on the amount of stimulus and guidance which may be provided. The 'head start' scheme in the USA has proved that the IQ of disadvantaged children can be raised in the early years by suitably improving their environment. Whether such improvement is maintained into later years is a subject of controversy between those psychologists who are pure environmentalists and those who believe that IQ is 70% inherited. At present it appears to be usual in Britain for the first year of formal schooling (from age five to six) to be used almost entirely for 'acclimatisation', for the development of social behaviour and manual skills (art work) but for very little specifically intellectual development. Therefore this first year in school tends to belong to the period of infancy, rather than to formal education. This does, however, raise problems for the child who can read before going to school. The age of progress through education has varied through the centuries. At one time boys used to learn Latin and Greek (but not mathematics!) at a very early age, such as three years. Edward the Black Prince was said to have commanded an army in a victorious battle at the age of 15, an age at which modern youth is compelled to be still at school. (But more experienced generals may have kept an anxious eye on the tactics of the young prince!) This question of age of learning should be kept in mind in the discussion of 'school leaving age' and vocational training (see below). The idea that a child should not be compelled to take employment before a certain age is just as much a concession or 'luxury' as the idea that an adult should *enjoy* retirement after a certain age and equally contributes to the process of 'work sharing'. Before the industrial revolution children were occupied with a good deal of productive activity in the home and on the land: it was the conditions of work outside the family, in factories, mines and chimney sweeping, which brought child employment into disrepute on grounds of health and humanity, before the introduction of universal education. This is apt to be forgotten when the obvious objection to child employment is now the thought that 'he ought to be at school'.

When considering the curriculum requirements of formal education one must remember that the individual's abilities will have to be exercised in the context of the contemporaneous social order — not many can opt out of their society as completely as Gaugin did and still be such a success as to have a worldwide and lasting reputation. On the one hand basic education must include some 'cultural' subjects such as religion, history, literature and social geography, which are justified if they are aimed at aiding the individual to make judgments on matters involving human behaviour. Such matters involve questions in which experimental test is usually too costly or otherwise impracticable; and one then has to rely on study of past and present attitudes, the factors which have influenced them and the events which have followed. To complement this, there must be some training in basic skills and some learning of facts which provide a basis for everyday life and for vocational training. In principle all educational activity should be geared to exercising the brain to improve its power of logical thinking and its unique powers of associative and innovative thinking. (A computer can function logically; but its power of associative thinking, of spotting previously undetected analogies, is negligible and its power of innovation arguably nil.) Before British money was decimalised there was a noticeable difference between shop assistants in small shops in England and in France. In England the shop assistant could often do the necessary arithmetic mentally — with farthings, pence and shillings — whereas in France the items to be added would always be written down. (The French did realise, however, that a decimal system made it easy to calculate 10% for service! The same idea did not seem to catch on when VAT in Britain was 10%.) Now we are all levelled by the adding cash register, together with the electronic weighing machine which gives a direct reading of price per lot. An important question is whether the elimination of practice in mental agility by these mechanical aids leads to a deterioration in general mental ability, as measured by IQ. There used to be a story of an engineer who reached for his slide rule to find that 2 x 2 was approximately 3.99: perhaps the realistic modern equivalent would be the person who reaches for an electronic calculator to add, say, 23 and 47. Certainly a positive attitude of looking for solutions to problems, or ways round them, is helpful; and this is inherent in the practice of 'short cuts' in arithmetic. Note 1 to Chapter 6 mentioned the increase in IQ in Japan, for which there is no accepted explanation. One can only suggest, as a pure speculation, that there might be a connection with education though the psychologists are unwilling to speculate, insisting on waiting for proof or sufficient evidence. But in the real world we cannot afford to wait before trying to improve the situation, so we must speculate.

An extreme antithesis of the 'want to learn' approach has been reported from California.[5] This report is from Garfield High School which is in a poor, Spanish-speaking, neighbourhood in East Los Angeles where the community is one of large families and low incomes, with no great love for education. Remarkable success has been achieved in a national test in calculus (administered by the

Educational Testing Service) by what has been described as a killing routine. Each lesson started with a five-minute test and pupils did two hours of after-school work each school-day and four hours of homework at the weekend. But one must beware that the good results which were obtained by this method might have been due in part to what may be called 'the Hawthorne effect'. In the late 1920's the Western Electric Company experimented on the effect of working conditions on productivity at the Hawthorne plant: and in a control experiment found that a subsequent *deterioration* in working conditions led to a *further improvement* in output. The explanation is that workers improved their output *because they knew they were the subject of an experiment*. Similarly the pupils may have responded to the novelty of the situation, though one would not normally have taken their co-operation for granted. This would then be another example under the general heading of 'motivation', though the fact remains that one cannot learn a subject like mathematics without hard work. A negative feature of the whole affair is that education in other subjects must surely have suffered as a result of the amount of work put into this particular branch of mathematics. None the less, it shows that 'old fashioned' methods can achieve striking results.

The effect of motivation, of whatever kind, is certainly very powerful. This brings us to the point that it is essential to inculcate a will to succeed in some role. It must be made clear that nobody need be a plain drop-out, though everyone has the right to adopt a life-style other than the current norm of society, provided it is in some way purposeful. The author once illustrated this point in an open letter to a class of university students on the following lines: 'I do not mind if you wish to be a poet or a politician, but no-one will respect you unless you make a success of *something*. Unless you have some alternative in mind, you had better make a success of the university course (in Electronic Engineering) on which you have embarked.'

A possible compromise between learning by rote and relying on the will to learn is described by the 'plastering' metaphor in which the untrained mind is likened to a bare framework which is to be covered with plaster: when plaster is thrown at it, some will fall off but some will stick until eventually the whole is covered. Another useful metaphor is 'opening windows', meaning introducing the pupil to hitherto unknown ideas and fields of thought.

Basic education shades into vocational training on the one hand and academic education on the other. (The term 'academic' is used for advanced non-vocational education rather than 'further' or 'higher' because these two terms have very specific connotations in the present organisation of education in Britain.) The existence of an IQ distribution is assumed (on the same basis as in Chapter 6, namely that it is an experimental fact, regardless of the reasons for it) and therefore it is assumed that only a minority will go on to academic education. Empirically the border line is the end of compulsory education; and that in practice only a minority in Britain continue is apparent from the current arguments about the size of school needed to support a sixth form or the desirability of a sixth-form college serving several schools.

Can one then specify a core curriculum for basic education in the new era? The 'three R's' (reading, writing and arithmetic) will still be of fundamental importance. It is sometimes suggested that with television presenting information pictorially and with computers both accepting spoken input and giving output by synthetic speech, reading and writing will no longer be necessary. (The use of synthetic speech for communication between automobile devices and the driver is a special case, because it enables the driver to receive additional information while continuing to concentrate his vision on the road.) It is nonsense to suggest that reading and writing will not be used in future. The printed word will for a long time remain the most convenient and economic way of storing information in a form which is immediately and universally accessible. Such information ranges from a book through the instructions for the use of a relatively complex piece of apparatus like a camera to instructions for opening the door of an emergency exit. (One serious air crash may have been due to a baggage handler's failure to read the instructions for *closing* a hatch, though the fact that the consequences were so disastrous was also regarded as a fault in the design of the aircraft.) If you can read, you should also be able to write — at least with a word processor! A new issue arises here, as to whether correct (i.e. customary) spelling and grammar are necessary. Both may be necessary to some extent to avoid ambiguity. In spelling, roll in mistake for role is well known; the author has also recently seen poll in place of pole. Carelessness in word order and in arrangement of dependent clauses can cause ambiguity while correct use of inflections can aid clarity. (The English language has comparatively few inflections and some of these, like 'who' and 'whom' are often ignored.) On the same argument as was used above on non-decimal currency and mental arithmetic, the idiosyncracies of English spelling may be a blessing in disguise. There is a tendency in some quarters to take the view that self-expression (in writing) must not be hampered by undue attention to spelling and grammar. The first point is that any kind of expression is useless if it is not sufficiently clear and unambiguous to be understood by others. But a more fundamental point is that self-expression is not synonymous with creativity: an insistence on disciplined expression need not destroy creativity.

Turning to the third 'R', the idea of replacing arithmetic by mathematics (the 'new maths') is misguided. The pocket electronic calculator, which is thought to have eliminated arithmetic, provides a quick way of doing some calculations* but it is also a quick way of making mistakes. One should not put a problem though the calculator without making a rough estimate of the answer independently, so as to know whether the answer from the calculator is acceptable. (This is not always possible when using a large computer for complex calculations, but the inclusion of checks on correctness is part of the art of writing computer programs.) All electronic computers work internally on a binary scale of arithmetic which can be used to illustrate the important mathematical principle that arithmetic need not be based on a unique scale, such as decimal, but which is of no significance to the ordinary user since calculators and computers are programmed to accept input and deliver output in decimal form. The internal binary scale is of no more importance to the user than is the electronic working of the silicon chips. On the other hand, the *program* is the link between the user and the computer, and so an introduction to the notations and conventions of computer-programming languages is desirable, though one is embarrassed by the multiplicity of programming languages in use at present. But having learnt one of the many languages makes it easier to learn another when needed. For large applications, e.g. for payroll or for stock control in a large factory, one can buy a ready-made program; but it may not suit one's individual requirements without modification. The program may also need periodical up-dating: payroll program will need modifying to take account of the recent change in sick-pay rules. The spread of cheap personal microcomputers will stimulate the learning of programming outside the educational system. There should, however, be no departure from the teaching of traditional arithmetic as part of basic education. Mathematics proper belongs to academic education, though a little of it may well be introduced fairly early. Geometry is a special case because Euclid lived at a time when quantitative measurement was difficult. His propositions (or theorems) are therefore exercises in the logical deduction of varied results from a minimum number of axioms. As such they may be used as an exercise in logical thinking.

There is at present a drive to get computers into schools, so that pupils can have 'hands on' experience. This is useful in order to encourage a reasonable attitude to computers. But the essential feature in the present state of technology is the dependence of man-machine communication on the *keyboard*, borrowed from the typewriter. This may not last for ever, but for the present ability to use a keyboard is as important as the ability to write — some of us hope more important than the ability to write elegantly. There is also computer-aided education which may have several advantages. The novelty factor may hold interest, i.e. it adds to motivation; a rebuke from the computer for a wrong answer can be tactful and more readily accepted than a rebuke from a human teacher; the learning process is self-paced; and finally the program might have been devised by someone of higher qualifications and experience than could be expected from a local teacher. But on the other hand the loss of human contact should be a disadvantage; and the compromise for the younger age groups is that computer-aided education should be an aid, not a substitute, for the human teacher. At university level, however, there is evidence that in come subjects students learn better from a computer-aided sequence than from conventional lectures, presumably due to the last two of the advantages. We have now an 'inverted' situation in which children may know more than their parents about computers. Regardless of the extent to which computers are provided in schools, the spread of cheap micro-computers in the home will reinforce this state of affairs, since the home computer plus video games may be regarded as an expensive toy. One has every sympathy with demands from teachers to be given instruction in the characteristics and uses of computers in order to keep up with their pupils.

We are now merging into academic education. The difference between 'basic' and 'academic' education is often said to be that the latter pursues subjects 'in greater depth', a metaphorical phrase of which the meaning is not too clear. It is sometimes taken to mean 'in greater detail' but while this is relevant it should not be the whole criterion. Broadly speaking, basic education has to be content with presenting the facts while academic education aims also at an understanding of causes. The author's personal experience relates mainly to academic education in mathematics and physical science: the absence of detailed reference to the humanities must not be taken to imply that similar arguments could not be mounted in their case also. There comes a time when a topic which was previously only of specialised application comes into vocational training for so many different occupations that it might as well be pulled back into general education at the appropriate level. It was for this reason that an introduction to programming notation and methods was included in basic education, together with arithmetic, while most of mathematics proper was reserved for 'academic' education which in Britain means school sixth form, college of further education, polytechnic or university. Mathematics is an immensely extensive logical structure — so extensive that no one person is master of all of it** — which has been built up on a minimum number of axioms. From this structure there can be derived a number of *mathematical techniques* which have found specific application in science and engineering; and when use of a particular technique has become sufficiently widespread, e.g. use of elementary algebra and of the differential calculus, teaching of this technique is brought into the school level of academic education. Geometry has already been mentioned as a special case, and trigonometry also deserves mention. It was originally concerned with relations between sides and angles of triangles and was essential to surveying. (The concrete mountings for theodolites which are found on hill summits are commonly known as 'trig. points'), but angle functions such as sine and cosine play an extensive part in the alternating–current technology of electrical power and electronic engineering. The past half century has seen many additional pieces of mathematical technique come into use by professional engineers and physicists so that such topics as vector algebra, manipulation of matrices and the Fast Fourier Transform (FFT) can now come into their university undergraduate curricula.

Vocational training is usually regarded as a post–school activity designed to meet the needs of industry. The most controversial question is that of discipline, which tends to be more strict (and more formalised, thanks to trade unions and 'employment protection' legislation) in industry than in schools. It has long been a tenet of the theory of management that the acceptance of orders should be obtained on the basis of the subordinate understanding that the action ordered is necessary, rather than on the basis of 'because I say so'.[1] In practice this precept may be varied for two opposite reasons. On the one hand it may demand an amount of time and patience, to explain the situation, which the superior does not have. On the other hand, the subordinate may feel 'if the boss says so I will do it, because the boss is usually right'. Unfortunately the latter attitude is not common in large enterprises and a source of deteriorating industrial relations is the use of, or implication of, 'because I say so or else ...' which is likely to be met with an unspoken 'I will do it this time but ...'. The existence of trust in industrial relations is a major factor in the success of any enterprise (whether private or nationalised) and the possibility of its attainment is affected by attitudes developed at school. Pupils should ideally have a genuine respect for teachers which would lead to co-operation in all types of school work and activity; and this spirit of co-operation in school may be carried forward to co-operation in industrial enterpres if suitably encouraged. In unfortunate cases, however, pupils give only grudging obedience to authority and regard the representatives of authority as a hostile group — 'them' in opposition to 'us'. This attitude also may be carried forward when the authority is management in industry instead of teachers in school and such an attitude of hositlity militates against good industrial relations. Some ideas about management and about the economics of industry must be included in all vocational training. Discipline is regarded as unpleasant in itself but it is not always possible to achieve desirable ends without going through unpleasant procedures and discipline (preferably self-discipline) is necessary to ensure acceptance of the unpleasantness. It is usually agreed that some discipline is necessary to ensure that the freedom of the individual does not destroy the happiness of others and to make possible co-operation or teamwork. Discipline is highly formalised in the rules of games and to some extent this justifies the saying that 'the battle of Waterloo was won on the playing fields of Eton'. What industry (and society) most needs now and in the future are reliability and responsibility, both of which involve self-discipline. By reliability is meant the certainty that if a task is undertaken it will be completed properly. Responsibility is illustrated by the attitude that 'if something is wrong, I must do something about it'. These traits will be especially important in the factory of the future, where the functioning of the whole will depend on the activities of a small number of maintenance workers who will be key personnel.

Logical thinking and a facility for association of ideas are also important in 'trouble shooting', i.e. the diagnosis and remedying of unforeseen breakdowns. Routine or preventive maintenance should minimise the frequency of such occurrences, but if an unforeseen malfunction does occur it must be remedied quickly.

Some commercial and industrial activities, e.g. the whole sphere of private and public administration (together with such functions as marketing) will be comparatively little affected by automation, although computers will be used and some technical activities within these spheres will be changed. We have already seen shorthand largely displaced by audio typing; and the 'secretarial' courses of the future will have to include instruction in the use of word processors and electronic mail. The academic education associated with administration, the formulation and carrying out of policies which involve wider than scientific values, is a long-standing problem. On the one hand it is argued that the 'humanities', the study of classical or modern cultures and literatures in the native language of the people concerned lead to an understanding of human behaviour. On the other hand, no-one can be considered well-educated who does not know something of physical and biological science. As a sign of the increasing emphasis on science, the saying that 'the pen is mightier than the sword' might now be replaced by 'the television screen is mightier than the hydrogen bomb'. An example of a more radical effect of technology on a non-scientific occupation is in accounting. Since so much of the bookkeeping and analysis is now performed by computers, the modern auditor must have a good understanding of computer programming if he is to be really satisfied about the destination of every sum of money — to be able to establish the 'audit trail'. One of his functions should be to detect or prevent computer crime. (He might prevent it by suggesting better safeguards in the computer program.) It is increasingly possible for someone within the computer staff of a large enterprise to steal money of the order of a million pounds by manipulation of the computer program. (Embezzlement on this scale makes exploits like The Great Train Robbery seem clumsy.) The more people are educated in computer programming, the greater the risk of someone succumbing to criminal temptation, and the greater the importance of auditors understanding what is done and can be done.

There are already in existence various courses which provide a good deal of vocational training for the technologies employed in industry a rough definition of 'professional' and 'technician' being that the professional makes the rules or develops new procedures but the technician works according to existing rules and procedures, though using intellectual as well as manual skills . The professional level is catered for increasingly by university courses leading to an honours degree,[2] though in some cases there is a possibility of promotion from technician to professional level. Engineering technicians are at present drawn partly from the less academically successful university graduates — particularly those with pass degrees — and partly from specialised technician courses. At present the word 'technician' tends to have a particularly scientific and engineering connotation but the provision of vocational training for all must in future include 'technician level' courses for all occupations, with a particular eye to the 'service' occupations which will provide the majority of employment opportunities in future. Some courses already exist (without the 'technician' label) as exemplified by catering, hotel management and agriculture. Obvious needs are office management, with the prospect of word processors etc.; printing and publishing, including graphic arts and methods of reproduction; automobile servicing including diagnostics and tuning (increasingly important with legislation on exhaust pollution); the construction industry including electrical installation, heating (with economy), lighting and ventilation; transport; communications; health services; glass and ceramics; clothing; food processing. (Some of these may already be covered to varying extents by existing courses.)

A universal scheme of vocational training also has to cater for those at the levels hitherto known as skilled manual (or craft), semi-skilled and unskilled. It has been reported that a Japanese shipbuilding firm has claimed that it does not employ any unskilled workers and has attributed the skilled status of its workers to education. A serious investigation of this Japanese claim would be worthwhile as part of a study to see how far IQ *can* be raised by education. There are two possibilities which need to be examined.

(i)   The claim may not be relevant to IQ but may mean that the firm's work is so organised as to make good use of those of limited capability.

(ii) The claim may be true of large firms but the less able go to smaller firms, just as large Japanese firms provide lifetime employment but their subcontractors do not.

But in the West we are faced with a distribution of IQ as a present fact, whatever may be achieved in future. If we then take the known IQ distribution as a crude method of classifying the population (see Chapter 6) the approximate estimates of the volume of vocational training provision of the several types are as shown in Table 15. A work-force of 21.9 million is assumed for future retiring and starting ages, corresponding to 25 million at present. (This figure is certainly not exact, since the 25 million includes about one-third of women who already retire at 60 and may not work continuously from 16 to 60. But it will give an idea of the numbers involved.) The distribution of IQ in the work-force is assumed to be the same as in the population as a whole, namely gaussian (or 'normal law of errors') with a mean value of 100 and standard deviation of 15. The relationship between IQ and level of occupation is similar to that discussed in Note 2 to Chapter 6. In line with the assumption that there will in future be little employment for the completely unskilled, and the Government's acceptance of MSC proposals that a one-year course of training should be available to every school leaver, the lowest starting age has been taken as 17 (for a school leaving age of 16). The retiring age is taken as 60 for both men and women (as recommended in Chapter 7). The 'annual output' is obtained by dividing the number of persons at a particular vocational level by the length of working life at that level. The numbers requiring initial vocational training are not affected by unemployment, but there may be additional numbers from mid-life re-training, whether these are in or out of employment when the re-training is necessary.

If it is assumed that practically all at professional level, and rather less than half those at technician level, pass through tertiary[†] education (this would raise the average starting age of technicians) the total output of tertiary education would have to be about 100,000 graduates p.a. With an average length of course of 3.5 years (in England the traditional 3 years plus an allowance for some 4-year courses and some weaker students repeating a year) this would mean 350,000 students in tertiary education in Britain, which is the sort of figure which has been suggested at various times. A higher figure would probably be suggested by those who urge that university students should be more representative of the whole population in terms of class, sex and race, but this implies a different and undefined view of the appropriate 'qualification' for a university course. The remaining output of technicians, about 45,000 per annum, would

IQ RANGE	Occupation Level	% of total	Number out of 21.9 million	Starting age	Working life years	Annual output
Above 120	Professional	9	2.0 million	22	38	52,600
110–120	Technician	16	3.5 million	19	41	85,400
95–109	Average worker	38	8.3 million	17	43	193,000
80–94	"Unskilled"	28	6.1 million	17	43	141,900
Below 80	(Special needs)	9	2.0 million	17	43	46,500

The numbers which may be expected at various levels of vocational training.

Table 15

have to come from courses specially designed for them, of a wide variety as outlined above.

The main problem is that a scheme of universal vocational training will have to cater also for those below technician level who have been known as skilled manual (craft), semi-skilled and unskilled. It can be seen from Table   that together these may be expected to amount to about two-thirds of the work-force, and most of the employment opportunities for them will be in service industries. For some years there will continue to be a demand for engineering skills, though on a diminishing scale. Symptomatic of this diminution is the dispute within the AUEW (Amalgamated Union of Engineering Workers) in 1982 as to whether numerically-controlled machine tools should be operated by craftsmen (whose craft skill is rendered largely super-fluous by the numerical control) or by technician members of the same union. The decision in favour of the craftsmen, coupled with their training in programming the new machines, could well have been motivated by job preservation though there are possible technical arguments. It must be remembered that computer pro-gramming in general does not require a high level of mathematical knowledge: the requirement was once described as 'bright young people, the sort who are good at playing bridge'. More is required of the higher grade called 'systems analysts' but again not primarily mathematical skill. The nearest academic equivalent, at the *research* level, is 'artificial intelligence' and a university graduate in Computer Science might well become a systems analyst (perhaps on the way to becoming a management consultant).

This points to the general principle that vocational training can only build on the foundation provided by the combination of innate skills and general education, and should not rely on specialised education. It is fortunate that mental skills and attitudes, which will become increasingly important in the future, are generally adaptable to different tasks. An example of what is meant by a desirable mental attitude is embodied in the advice to students to regard an examination as a battle of wits between the student and the examiner. (Scrutiny of previous papers in search of standard types of question is a legitimate tactic, which the examiner tries to frustrate by varying the questions.) This approach, both in preparation and on the day, contrasts with plodding through whatever tuition is offered and eventually reading the examination questions with resignation (or despair).

Manual skills are less adaptable because (like athletic performance) they depend partly on innate ability and partly on development by praçtice. The purpose of vocational training is therefore two-fold. It is firstly to provide a certain amount of instruction and a great deal of practice in some skill which is at the time relevant to a particular type of employment, but is not of sufficiently widespread application to be included in general education. Note that *practice* of the skill is included but this will not always be accepted as equivalent to *experience*, partly because of inevitable differences between the training situation and the situation in production. The trouble is that a skill which is relevant at a particular time may cease to be relevant before the expiry of the 40 years or so of working life. The possible, indeed probable, need for retraining at a later date puts a premium on adaptability and the quality of general education. Secondly vocational training must provide an entry to a career for those who have not a very strong inclination towards any particular career. This will apply particularly to those who at present would be classified as semi-skilled or unskilled and have therefore had no formal vocational training. At the present time craft courses must be spread over a wide range of expertise, much as suggested for technician level courses, and with an eye particularly to service and non-manufacturing industries.

The semi-skilled may come from the lower ranks of the 'craft' courses. But what about the unskilled for whom there will be a negligible amount of work in future manufacturing industry and who will be least fitted to work on their own initiative in a non-industrial environment? (Remember that before the industrial revolution the incompetent poor were estimated to be as many as 25% of the population.) These can be expected to come from 'the bottom of the heap' of school leavers and the first necessity may well be remedial work in very basic education (literacy and numeracy). As far as possible, however, they should also be 'exposed to' a variety of activities: sometimes an individual will be so attracted to a particular activity which had not been previously encountered that the resulting motivation will change the whole life style. 'Exposed to' means more than 'given a choice of' and the difference is important because often an individual will not know what is involved in an activity which has never been experienced. Some youngsters will have very determined ideas about the type of course which they desire, and they should be allowed to get on with it provided the desire is matched by relevant ability. For others the first part of the training course should be divided into several periods of a few weeks each in varied activities such as engineering crafts, looking after small livestock (bees, free-range poultry, rabbits, goats), woodworking (including carving), gardening/horticulture, hair-dressing, car maintenance, catering etc. before choosing a course of comprehensive training for a particular type of employment. Even one of the trial activities which do not lead to a livelihood at first may come in useful for a change of employment, a hobby or something to return to in retirement.

The provision of such an array of courses seems utopian, for it demands considerable resources in money and very great resources in men and women who are both skilled in the various topics, able to teach and willing to devote at least part of their time to passing on their skills to a future generation. On the other hand there is the possibility of breaking down training into groups of manageable size: training cannot be a mass-production process, a consideration which is particularly relevant to the lower levels where motivation may initially be inadequate. The acceptance by the Government that training should not be forced on the young unemployed may be a blessing in disguise if training courses are consequently started with smaller numbers than would be needed to cope with everyone.

Before and during the industrial revolution, vocational training and practical experience were joined through apprenticeship. During this century there has been a shift away from the attitude that apprenticeship was a privilege — for which a premium was paid in professional occupations — to the idea that apprenticeship is a kind of employment which deserves 'a living wage'. Before the Second World War it was common for the larger organisations to take on more trainees than the number to whom they expected to offer permanent employment and retain only the best for themselves. (This was certainly true of engineering apprenticeships and of certain universities which took on a number of 3-year assistant lecturers in excess of the number of permanent appointments they could offer at the end of the three years.) It was argued that this was a service both to those who got the training and to smaller establishments in the relevant industry who could then acquire trained manpower without having to provide the training. There is now a trend against this type of apprenticeship for four reasons.

(1) The belief in 'full employment' has led to the abolition by

employment protection legislation of the unqualified right to 'hire and fire'.

(2) Training can be expensive for the firm in terms of the use of experienced personnel for supervision.

(3) Trainees are costly to industry in terms of both wages and on-costs such as National Insurance. Such costs may not be acceptable when the profitability of British industry is already low.

(4) There is a feeling against young people being in any way financially dependent on (a burden on) their parents after leaving school.

At the professional level this fourth point has led to the disappearance of the practice of asking for premiums for professional training. None the less, some period of training or experience *in industry* will still be required as a bridge between off-the-job vocational training and employment in a particular enterprise. In 1980 in West Germany, 50% of school leavers entered a 3-year apprenticeship at a wage less than half that of a skilled worker. There was some assistance from the Government in the form of grants for training facilities but the greater part of the costs was met by employers. The assumption in Britain at the moment, on the other hand, is that vocational training should be mostly in Government-funded education and training establishments. One compromise would be through a sandwich scheme. In France from 1st January 1982, persons up to the age of 23 and older people who have been employed for less than two years in the preceding five years can take part in a scheme known as 'alternance'. The aim is to provide systematic training at various levels in occupations by progressing through alternating periods of education/study and work training/experience and the scheme is to be funded by Government grants and revenue from increased taxes on employers.[††]

The initial training can be expected to provide the skills required for 10 or more years, but later a change of occupation may be necessary, particularly if the initial skills were related to manufacturing industry. But change of occupation may call for change of place of employment; and one of the problems is the geographical immobility of workers below the professional and technician levels, as discussed in Chapter 6. When computers have been installed to handle clerical work, it has been found that some of the existing clerical staff can be trained to take over the computer operations while the surplus can be lost through 'natural wastage', either directly or via transfer to other parts of the organisation. (Clerical staff usually includes a fair proportion of women of child-bearing age.) But what happens when the conversion of an engineering factory to robot operation reduces the shop–floor work–force to 5% of its previous number? The 5% required for supervision and maintenance can be selected from the original work–force and are happy to have more varied and responsible work; but what happens to the other 95%?

The French 'alternance' scheme of vocational training, which would be called in Britain a sandwich scheme, is open to anyone who has been unemployed for at least three years out of the past five. But is it necessary to impose such a harsh test if skills lose their employment value as a result of technological change? Something is needed to deter the 'perpetual student' who might only be concerned to obtain a year's subsistence on a free course: perhaps there might be a requirement to commute some part of redundancy payment. But what must be emphasised is that at levels below technician the usual requirement in the foreseeable future will not be for training in new techniques in the same industry but rather for training to enable the worker to move from a production industry to a service industry. Of course any who are able and willing to set up in business on their own, and so withdraw from the general employment market, should be encouraged to do so by facilities such as premises and loan capital at a low rate of interest. The meticulous attention to detail and sense of responsibility which is necessary for success in any self–employed enterprise is also more important for employees in service industries than in manufacturing industries because they may have more contact with consumers rather than with the higher echelons of their own employing organisation. There may be some radical changes of occupation — for example in moving from manufacturing industry to distribution — but one can often build on past experience. A knowledge of the design and manufacture of a product can be useful in the marketing and servicing of a similar product. The point which must be accepted, however, is that a working life of some 40 years may not be spent entirely in one occupation; and this is likely to be especially true during the next few years (or decades) while the transition from 'manned' factories to 'robot–operated' factories is taking place.

Then there is the question of filling the retirement years. A politician who had just lost high office was asked whether he expected to return to public life and is reported to have said 'I do not intend to spend the rest of my life playing golf and walking on the beach.' The male expectation of life from age 60 was 16.0 years in 1979[4] and is probably increasing: this is too long a period to be spent in aimless existence. A minority will start some kind of self-employed enterprise and this is to be commended, because it adds to the economic activity (and therefore wealth) of the community with at most an indirect subtraction from total employment. It may in fact add directly to employment if it develops to such an extent as to have employees who are below retiring age. The assumption is that the self-employed enterprise will usually contribute to the community something which was not previously being provided, thereby adding a new kind of wealth without interfering with existing wealth/employment relationships. Another minority will have sufficient financial resources to indulge their particular interests in such things as travel or the arts. For most, however, the need is for some form of purposeful activity which does not require substantial expenditure. In some cases this need can be met by a 'profitable' hobby, which will at least yield enough return to cover expenses. But all of those concerned have by definition a life-time's experience in their own individual trades and they could therefore make a great contribution in their specialities to the community. There is then a logical argument for shifting 'community service' from the young unemployed to the retired, or at least have the retired take over supervision and technical advice. There would be objection to the latter on the ground that the retired would be taking over supervisory jobs which might have been filled by full-time workers (even though community service is on work which could not be paid for on a commercial basis), so any such scheme might have to wait until unemployment has ceased to be an acute problem.

Another possible activity for the retired is further education, often in some subject not related to the past career. Unfortunately the present financial stringency in Britain is making the price of such courses rise sufficiently to deter some potential students.

Most activities cost some money, so there is a bias towards part-time employment, profitable hobbies or activities which pay expenses. The important factor is that the retired should have some aim or interest in life: this will tend to make them live longer and the resulting increase in the tax-payer's contribution to the cost of pensions on that account should be borne willingly!

Notes

* The ordinary (non-printing) pocket calculator is useful for multiplication and division; but it is unsuitable for adding a long column of figures because it gives no check of the number of items fed in, as mechanical calculators did, to warn if one had skipped any items.

** The author once consulted a professor of mathematics about an unusual problem and was told 'There is only one man in the country who can help you with that'.

† Degree courses at universities or elsewhere.

†† Information on West Germany and France is taken from 'A New Training Initiative'[3].

References

1. See, for example, *Dynamic Administration*, the collected papers of Mary Parker Follett, edited by Henry C. Metcalf and L. Urwick.

2. *Engineering Our Future* (The Finniston Report). HMSO, Cmnd 7794, January 1980.

3. *A New Training Initiative: A Programme for Action*. HMSO, Cmnd 8455, December 1981.

4. Registrar General, *Mortality Statistics 1978*, Series DH1 No. 6 HMSO 1982 (Table 23).

5. Hilary Wilce, Stricter maths teaching methods achieve 'miracle'. *Times Educational Supplement*, 31st December 1982, p.1.

Appendix

SOME CONTROVERSIAL QUESTIONS

As noted in the Preface, the economic prosperity of Britain depends on a number of factors besides the effect of technology on manufacturing industry. Unfortunately most of these are politically controversial; but some of them are reviewed below.

1. Low productivity.

There is no doubt that output per man–hour (and consequently the wage level) is much lower in UK industry than in several other industrial countries: the question is, why? The broadside from the political right is that it is due to shortcomings of the labour force, e.g. excessive tea breaks, union demarcation rules and other restrictive practices. The extreme of this view is illustrated by the joke about the visitor to a factory who asked 'How many people work here?' and received the answer 'About half'. It must, however, be recognised that restrictive practices had their origin in job–preservation. The counter to that policy is that if such practices make a firm inefficient (by international standards), then the firm will go out of business and *all* jobs will be lost. The broadside from the left is that it is due to industry being starved of investment, in effect a strike by capitalists, with the diversion of savings (particularly in pension and insurance funds) to property, government securities and investments abroad.

One counter to complaints about the work-force is that Japanese-managed factories in the UK seem to operate satisfactorily. Another is the remark of an American manager of a British factory: 'If there is anything wrong in my plant I guess it will be *my* fault'. The job of managers is to manage, though some UK managers would add 'if the unions would let us' and some people would add 'with the participation of the workers'. A fact which must be borne in mind particularly when making comparisons between different factories, is that it is fairly easy to establish good industrial relations in a unit of up to a few hundred employees but it is a different matter when there are thousands, as in a large steel works or mass–production automobile plant. However, the principles of good management are the same:²any order should be seen to be reasonable, i.e. it should be an instruction rather than 'because I say so', and the organisation should be seen to be moving steadily. Abrupt and apparently random changes of policy are unsettling and temporary lack of work is demoralising, whether the employee is laid òff or paid to do nothing. Some large plants suffer from the particular disadvantage that the work is unpalatable (the automibile assembly line has been a notorious example) and a feeling of dissatisfaction with the job can easily be turned into a feeling of hostility towards the management. At this point the author would like to make two pleas. The first is that management should be regarded as a profession requiring formal preparation, rather than as an occupation for ambitious amateurs who believe in 'flying by the seat of the pants'. (Has anyone ever thought of flying a 747 aircraft by the seat of his pants?) The second is that more consideration should be given to 'middle management' who have the duty of taking the policy laid down by top management and carrying it out with the co–operation of the work–force, a co-operation which they alone are in a position to ensure.

A sufficient reason for general reluctance to invest in British industry is that it has not been profitable. The Stock Exchange price level has nowhere near kept pace with inflation and the average percentage return on equities has been less than that on government securities. Therefore the motive for putting money into industry must in practice be the hope of capital gain in special cases, i.e. it has a strong speculative element. But the trend towards an egalitarian society has meant that large sums of money are not usually at the disposal of individuals but are in the hands of 'funds', particularly insurance and pension funds, of which the trustees feel obliged to *invest* (for a safe income and moderate capital gain) rather than speculate in the hope of a large capital gain. (Since the word 'speculate' carries some moral opprobrium, it is now common to talk of 'venture capital'.) None the less, it is widely said that there is no difficulty in getting money for a project which looks like being successful. But one of the difficulties is that someone with a good idea may not have the financial expertise to commercialise it successfully. A finance house will not look kindly on someone who does not present an adequate analysis of his sales prospects and cash flow requirements. (Even Rolls–Royce automobiles has been said to have been bankrupted because of inadequate financial management.) Some university engineering courses include business studies, a feature which has been recommended by the Finniston Committee of enquiry into the engineering profession in its report entitled 'Engineering our Future'.

2. Free Trade or 'Siege Economy'?

One of the difficulties of the British Government at the present time is the high proportion of manufactured goods in our imports; and the consequent fear is that any increase in consumer spending results in an increase in such imports, rather than an increase in employment in British manufacturing industry. (This is apart from, or additional to, the main theme of this book that manufacturing industry is increasingly able to increase its output without increasing employment.) Some say the obvious answer is to keep out imports (by tariffs or quotas) 'until British industry has had time to become efficient'. Since the Common Market is a free-trade area, this idea of putting a wall round Britain and retreating into a policy which opponents call 'the siege economy' inevitably leads to the issue of withdrawal from the Common Market. Opponents of such policy cite as tangible arguments against it firstly the probability of tariff retaliation by other countries and secondly objections to leaving the Common Market. Less tangible is the feeling that British industry might not in fact use the protection to raise its efficiency, particularly if the level of unemployment led to the provision of employment taking precedence over increasing efficiency.

A more subtle argument for protection is that the marginal cost of production is always less than the average cost, or it can be reckoned that the average cost falls as the quantity of production rises. If all the costs of development and other overheads are loaded on to the quantity of production which goes to the home market, then any extra produced for export appears to cost less and can therefore be sold more cheaply abroad. If this argument were pushed to the limit it would mean that consumers everywhere should logically buy imported goods rather than home production, unless there were some form of protection of home industry. It is alleged that some countries, both inside and outside the Common Market, do in fact restrict the flow of imports by non-tariff devices such as elaborate safety and quality regulations or tedious customs procedures and that the UK does not; and this would obviously be unfair to British producers.

A real factor is that in a time of widespread unemployment all countries are endeavouring to 'export unemployment' by manipulation of the balance of trade, leading to accusations of unfair subsidies and dumping. But one must recognise that some countries, e.g. in Eastern Europe, are so far in debt internationally that they can hardly be blamed for taking extreme measures to obtain 'hard' currency in order to avoid a financial default which some say would cause an international banking disaster. There is also the 'oil problem'. Japan, for example, must spend about half its export earnings on importing fuel. It gets its foreign currency by exporting electronic and engineering goods to industrialised countries, but must pay half the proceeds for fuel, largely to oil-exporting countries. It is therefore not surprising that Japan is reluctant to take imports from the industrialised countries of equal value to the exports to them. If it did, it would not be able to pay for fuel. The trouble is that most of the oil-exporting countries are not in a position to accept the Japanese type of export; and in the absence of sufficient three-cornered trade the net effect must be to pile up petro-dollars. There is, indeed, a three-cornered trade between Japan, USA and Australia (Australia supplying raw materials to Japan) which is at present suffering from a contraction of the US market for Japanese manufactured goods.

3. Government Spending

It is a doctrinaire belief of the Right that government spending is a *bad thing* and equally of the Left that it is a *good thing*. Much of the early infrastructure of the UK, e.g. canals, turnpike roads, railways and docks, was built up by private capital at a time when some men were rich enough to provide a significant part of the capital required; and the establishment of the principle of the limited liability company attracted the contribution of smaller amounts of venture capital by others. The motive was *profit*. Nowadays developments such as the electricity grid, with its associated power stations, and motorways are public undertakings with the aim of public service rather than profit. The trend towards a more equal distribution of wealth has been paralleled by the growth of the 'welfare state' and of communal amenities. Among the latter the most obvious recent examples are the spread of piped water, of electricity supply and the improvement of roads. (The author can remember country roads which were surfaced with local material and not tarmaced.) All this involves expenditure by the government, either central or local, and government expenditure inexorably increases.   As long as the GDP is rising, a constant level of taxation (i.e. a constant proportion of the GDP taken by the government) will yield a rising fund for government expenditure; and it has been suggested that the welfare state was financed for its first two decades in this way. The situation now is that if the GDP per capita in the UK were equal to that in some other industrialised countries, roughly twice its present value, there would be twice as much money available for government expenditure *without increasing the level of taxation.*

In 1982 the Treasury prepared economic forecasts for two scenarios, including estimates of future government spending on present policies but with the Public Service Borrowing Requirement (PSBR, in effect the budget deficit) brought down from its present 3½—4% of GDP to 2% of GDP. The existence of these forecasts was revealed in *The Times* of 30th June 1982 and they were discussed in detail in *The Times* of 7th October 1983, p.5. Scenario A assumed that productivity in the marketed sector of the economy would grow at 3% p.a. and GDP at 2.5% p.a., both relative to 1981 figures and that the rate of inflation would be 5% p.a. Scenario B assumed a growth in productivity of 1.5% and a GDP growth of 0.75% at first falling to 0.5% after 1986, with inflation at 10%. Unemployment, as well as inflation, would be higher for B than for A, but the foreign exchange rates would be about the same. In the less favourable scenario B taxes would need to be raised by about 50%; and this corresponds to an increase in taxes which might be, for example, either an income tax basic rate of 45p or VAT at 25%, plus a doubling of other excise duties (alcohol, tobacco, automobile licences etc.) or some of each. The present prospects for the UK economy may be between the two scenarios; but such scenarios, like all mathematical models of the economy, are mainly extrapolations of past trends with little allowance for *structural change,* the factor which is the only real hope for the UK economy.

4. Deficit Financing

There is a fair argument that (a) the National Debt (the sum of all past borrowing) should be allowed to increase in proportion to the increase in publicly owned assets (less depreciation!) and (b) in times of depression one should permit a budget deficit, with a compensating budget surplus in more prosperous times. A superficial objection to (a) is that the burden of interest payment will increase; but the GDP also increases, and as a proportion of the GDP the total government indebtedness (central plus local) is not increasing in the long term. The difficulty is that both (a) and (b) have to be covered by government borrowing (the Public Sector Borrowing Requirement) and the need to attract money into loans to the Government both raises interest rates and provides unwelcome competition with investment in industry. The alternative of issuing money or credit without countervailing loans is, in general, inflationary.

5. Interest rates

It has often been said recently that high interest rates were harming industry, both by discouraging investment in capital projects and by increasing the cost of working capital. But analysis of the published accounts of some large manufacturing companies suggests that the cost of borrowing in the normal course of business is not an outstanding factor in total expenditure. (The situation may be different in smaller companies, where there may also be a cash flow problem.) There is also a difference between nominal and real interest rates, the difference being equal to the rate of inflation. The real rate has on occasion been negative (hence the attraction of index-linked National Savings and treasury stock) and it is this real rate which should control capital investment and is of paramount concern to long-term investors such as pension funds. (It is not relevant to international lending, since exchange rates may be affected by other considerations besides inflation.) It has been suggested that the trend for industry to become more capital intensive would increase the demand for investment and so force up interest rates. However, continuing low interest rates in Switzerland confirm the established view that long term lenders are satisfied with a real return of 3–4%.

6. What is full employment?

The third difficulty is that since vacancies and job losses do not occur in matched pairs, there will be some unemployment while individuals who have lost jobs are waiting for vacancies to occur; and *average* rates of occurrence of vacancies and job losses would not tell us how much of this waiting there would be. It does, however, bring us into accord with the idea of the unemployed being a reserve of labour; and one can then estimate the minimum rate of unemployment as Beveridge did, though in the event his estimate was proved wrong over the period 1946 to 1966.

But there is also the problem of mismatch between vacancies and unemployed; a vacancy for a sheet metal worker in Birmingham is of no use to an unemployed fisherman in Hull. So now there is the further condition that an unemployed person may wait until a *suitable* vacancy arises. 'Suitable' may mean a job in the same occupation as before, in the same area and at a suitable wage. The unemployment which is caused by waiting for a suitable vacancy is known as *frictional* unemployment because it is not due to a lack of balance between job losses and vacancies but to the incidental difficulties of fitting the two together, just as the internal friction in a machine is separate from the fundamental equality of power input and work output.

Then there is the problem of *structural* employment. If the fisherman in Hull came from a deep sea trawler, he is unlikely to get another identical job: he will have to change his occupation to a greater or less extent as a result of the *structural* change in employment represented by the decline of the deep sea fishing industry.

A further complication is that according to Danils' survey (Chapter 5, Reference 7) somewhere near 40% of the unemployed in June 1981 could not show that they had been *forced* to leave their previous jobs. This is a difficult area because of the cases of employees leaving to avoid being dismissed and of employers making life difficult for employees whom they wished to lose. But there must have been a significant number who left their jobs voluntarily without having another job to go to.

This survey also mentions that the unemployed may reject jobs which are offered and that 56% of the jobs which were rejected were offered through the Jobcentres. Remembering that only one third of all vacancies are reported to Jobcentres, this suggests that employers used the Department of Employment services only for their less attractive jobs.

Some would argue that both voluntary unemployment and the rejection of jobs when offered are contrary to the spirit of 'genuinely seeking work'. But in relation to the rejection of jobs, it must be remembered that the much-publicised 'poverty trap' is real: a person taking a low-wage job may be no better off financially than on the dole with the various social security benefits available, and after taking account of the expenses of travel to work and so on, could even be worse off. Since some people (including Len Murray, in a BBC2 television programme on 1st January 1984) say that unemployment is not something for which the individual should feel any guilt, the unemployed person may further argue that if taking a job caused income to be increased by only a few pounds a week, it would not be worthwhile to work 40 hours for so little gain.

It was pointed out in Chapter 5 that Beveridge's concept of the unemployed as a reserve of labour was linked with the idea that such a reserve was necessary in order to avoid wage inflation. As industrial jobs become more specialised the definition of a 'suitable' job becomes more critical, so that frictional unemployment tends to increase. The counterpart of this is that an employer has difficulty in finding a person with exactly the skill he wants unless there is a large number of unemployed from whom to choose; and since deficiency in the size of the reserve causes wage inflation, the increasing complexity of occupations requires a larger reserve of unemployment (unless individuals show more adaptability to change of occupation). If one accepts some inflation but not accelerating inflation, one adopts the non-accelerating-inflation rate of unemployment (NAIR) which might now be 5% in contrast to the actual 1—2% unemployment of 1946—66. Although this would not be full employment in the 100% sense, it would represent the highest rate of employment which was consistent with a stable economy. It is hoped (one can say no more at present) that the NAIR could be below the present 12—13% rate of unemployment. It should be noted also that the role of wage inflation in the general inflation up to the end of 1982 is controversial; but one fact is that even in 1983 the rate of increase in wages has been greater than the rate of inflation.

7. Equality or inequality of incomes?

The trend since 1945 has been towards greater equality of incomes. It was pointed out in the text that in so far as expansion of service industries related to the maintenance of the infrastructure it would require increased taxation; and progressive taxation is a means towards equalisation of after-tax incomes. But expansion of personal services would require greater *inequality* of disposable income: one cannot employ the services of another if his/her wage is comparable with one's own income. It is not suggested that the number of incomes of 20 times the national average should be increased — anyway there are so few of them that it would not make much difference. But there is a case for more after-tax incomes of about 5 times the national average — say about £25,000 per annum at 1983 prices. This could, for example, allow competition with the cash-and-carry supermarket by the more expensive old-style grocer's shop with shop assistants and delivery service, giving more employment in the service sector. It would also make it feasible for more people to employ someone at the average wage, at least part-time, for personal service. Such an increase in disposable incomes would only be possible through a greatly increased productivity in 'productive' industry, since all service industries must be paid for by the industries which produce goods for sale at home and abroad, including 'invisible exports' and things like computer software. There would also have to be avoidance of the style of 'productivity bargaining' in which much of the profit from productivity is taken by the residue of the shop-floor workers.

But perhaps the drive for egalitarianism has gone too far to be reversed.

8. Why 1966?

Unemployment started a rising trend about 1966 and an obvious comment on this is to indicate that redundancy payments started in December 1965 and ERS (the earnings related supplement to unemployment benefit, paid after two weeks and up to six months' unemployment) commenced in October 1966. The Department of Employment set up a working party, with representation from the Institute of Manpower Studies, the Department of Applied Economics of Cambridge University and the National Institute of Economic and Social Research, as well as the Department of Employment, to investigate this point. The report of the working party is summarised in the Department of Employment Gazette for October 1976, pages 1093 to 1099. They found that neither redundancy payments nor the earnings related supplement could have affected numbers significantly and that the rise in unemployment after 1966 was consistent with the decline in employment. On the other hand, they found that the pattern of relationships between vacancies and unemployment changed significantly after 1966 *for men but not for women*. It might be argued that women would be less affected by ERS, owing to their lower usual wage, so the sex difference seems to point in favour of ERS being involved. One would expect the group with unemployment lasting between 8 and 26 weeks to be most affected by ERS; but an independent plot of the percentage of the total (men and women) who were unemployed 8—26 weeks against vacancies, shows no change of pattern around 1966. This was not an oil crisis year and there is no reason to think that automation suddenly took effect: the ideas had been around for more than ten years and in any case one would expect a more gradual change.'

Comparison with other countries tends to suggest a general cause rather than one peculiar to the UK. The OECD has carried out a comparison of unemployment in 15 countries, including the USA, UK, West Germany and Sweden, over the years 1966—83; and of these four, Sweden is the only one which does *not* show a rising trend prior to 1981.

Since different countries use different methods of recording unemployment (for example, the UK does not record the self-employed who are out of work), the OECD made some adjustments to national figures in order to arrive at a standardised basis for their figures. It is noticeable that from 1967 to 1977 the OECD figures for the UK were higher than our national published figures, e.g. 3.3% against 2.3% in 1967, but since 1979 the difference has been small.

An important feature is the *duration* of unemployment. The percentage of male unemployed who remained unemployed for longer than eight weeks has been taken as a rough measure of this. This percentage rose steadily from 56% in 1967 to 71—72% over the years 1976—80 and then rose sharply to 81% in 1982. Thus the year of peak output, 1976, showed a substantial increase in the duration of unemployment compared with 1967. The sharp rise during a period of unprecedentedly high unemployment (1982) is to be expected; but the gradual rise in duration may be either effect or cause of the gradual rise in total unemployment. The cause of the sudden change in the pattern of unemployment versus vacancies in 1966 has not been established.

GLOSSARY

Automation 'Mechanisation' can be defined as the replacement of human muscle power, and to some extent human manual skill, by machine power with human supervision and guidance. 'Automation' means that the human *guidance* is no longer required, the machine performing its task automatically, though a certain amount of supervision may still be required. In full automation (e.g. the factory operated by robots) the supervision is minimal, being limited to maintenance, the rectification of any breakdown which may occur and the re-programming of the machines for a different task. Silicon-chip–based microprocessors and robots facilitate full auto-mation because they can store complex information, respond also to information coming in from sensors and carry out complex tasks without human intervention.

Binary scale We are so familiar with the 'place' system on the decimal scale, where the same symbol in different places in a sequence of symbols represent number of units, tens, hundreds etc., that one has to go back to Roman numerals to realise that the 'place' system of numerals is not inevitable but is very advantageous. The first point is that the difference in signifi-cance between places need not be a power of ten but may be a power of *any* number, provided only that one has that number of symbols to choose from for each place. In the binary scale, which is used in the internal workings of computers for engineering rather than mathematical reasons, the successive places represent units, twos, fours, eights etc.; and whereas decimal fractions are tenths, hundredths, thousandths etc., binary fractions are halves, quarters, eighths, sixteenths etc. Only two symbols are needed, to represent nought and one, since one moves to the next higher place when the count reaches two, and it is usual to employ the familiar symbols 0,1. The idea of scales other than decimal is important in *mathematics* but is not essential in *arithmetic*.

Bits and bytes During the earlier part of the 1939—45 war much use was made of mechanical devices for performing calculations, for example to guide the aiming of anti–aircraft guns, because it was said that electrical devices were like gear wheels with rubber teeth — you could never be sure of the exact position. This applied to *analogue* devices in which some electric current or voltage had to be exactly proportional to a number. This changed when it was realised that any number could be defined by a sufficient number of yes/no decisions — on the binary scale in fact. One such decision, which is the unit of measurement on the binary scale, is a 'binary digit', or in abbreviated form a *bit*.

The simple teleprinter used five bits to denote any letter or numeral but the code now in general use employs seven bits so as to cover punctuation signs etc. as well as letters and numbers; and in operation within a computer system one often adds a further bit as a check against errors. A group of bits, usually eight in number, is then called a *byte* and the storage capacity associated with a computer may be measured in bytes instead of bits. This applies particularly to computers for commercial work, rather than scientific work, where much text may have to be stored in addition to numbers.

A side effect of working in binary digits is that in computer work the symbol 'k' associated with a number, e.g. 64k, means not 1,000 but $2^{10} = 1,024$.

CAD/CAM or CAE In addition to the use of computers to design the intricate and complex patterns of components and connections on small silicon chips (especially for LSI and VLSI) it is possible to use a computer and visual display unit (VDU) to replace the traditional drawing board for the design of mechanical components which are large enough to handle. In either case the method is known as computer–aided design (CAD). At the same time there is growing use of computers to control the subsequent process of manufacturing: initially there was only the direct computer control of machine tools (instead of the computer preparation of tapes which have to be fed to independent, numerically controlled machines) but now there is also computer control of the movement of work from one machine to another and of the whole flow of work

through the factory. This is called computer–aided manufacture (CAM). But there is no need for the two computers to
be separated. If the two computers are combined, or at least
can communicate with each other without human intervention, the result is computer–aided design *and* manufacture
(CAD/CAM). The computer control can be extended to
supply the raw materials and handling of finished products
and justifies the title 'computer–aided engineering' (CAE). It is
preferable for CAE to be developed *ad initio* as an integrated
system, or else as a set of linked modular systems, to avoid risk
of incompatibility between the CAD and the CAM parts.

Current Cost Accounting (CCA). The published accounts of a company
are required to give a true and fair view of its state of affairs.
('Fair' here has the sense of 'just' rather than 'of pleasing
appearance'.) But in times of high inflation the fair view is not
apparent if the various figures are based on prices which were
relevant some years before the date of the accounts. The most
obvious factor, depreciation, has been dealt with in Note 6 to
Chapter 4. In addition there are the points that materials used
in the current batch of products may have to be replaced at a
higher price, and that more monetary working capital may be
needed to cover higher prices all round: the CCA adjustments
are known as 'cost of sales adjustment' (COSA) and 'monetary
working capital adjustment' (MWCA).

One other factor, 'gearing adjustment' (GA), is not solely
and simply dependent on inflation. In the simplest case the
capital of a company is the amount subscribed initially for
shares; but if the management needs more money, or is
confident that it could profitably use more money in the
business, it may borrow money so tht the total capital is greater
than that subscribed by shareholders (plus retained profits,
which in principle belong to shareholders) and the ratio of
total capital to shareholders' capital is called the 'gearing'.
Companies often like to express their profits as so much per
share, but in CCA only a proportion of profit, equal to their
proportion of the total capital, is attributed to shareholders;
and this proportioning is called 'gearing adjustment'.

Education: primary, secondary, further and tertiary. The following is a
brief outline of the present (1984) organisation of education in

England. Education is compulsory from age 5 to 16, a statutory requirement which is fairly thoroughly enforced. The stage from 5 to 11, called 'primary', is conducted in local schools having a few hundred pupils (less in rural areas) while secondary schools, usually of the type called 'comprehensive' because they accept all children without any test of ability, are for age 11 to 16 and often have up to two thousand pupils. A small number of pupils attend fee–paying schools which are independent of the state system, the longer established of which are (misleadingly) called 'public schools'. These were largely boarding schools originally, the day schools which are comparable being 'grammar schools': and the feature which is common to both (apart from fees) is that entrance depends on passing an examination.

Those who stay at one of the types of secondary school beyond the age of 16, usually until 18, are mainly those aiming at entering tertiary education, which is at university level. Universities grant degrees by authority of royal charters, while the Council for National Academic Awards (CNAA) accredits courses for the award of degrees at other institutions. The CNAA was originally concerned with degree courses in technical subjects in the more advanced technical colleges but now also covers a wide spread of subjects in polytechnics. The latter are in principle equal in status with universities, but are controlled by local education authorities and are expected to have a curriculum with a more practical bias.

'Further education' (FE) is for those who are over the age of 16 but who have not stayed in a secondary school. It serves those who leave school at 16 but either then or later wish to return to education, possibly with the intention of acquiring qualifications by examination. ('Adult education' has in the past been mainly part–time and not directed towards examinations. The latter characteristic has become less universal since the establishment of the Open University.)

One further institution is the College of Education which has the function of training school teachers in the theory and practice of education at school level, together with some advanced study of subject matter. The basic course lasts three years, but the more able students can continue for a fourth year in order to obtain the degree of Bachelor of Education, which is usually conferred by arrangement with a neighbouring university. Correspondingly a university graduate, with a Bachelor's degree in a particular subject after three years, may take a fourth year to obtain the Certificate in Education and so become fully qualified to teach in a secondary school.

Group production The usual method of automobile manufacture employs an assembly line for the assembly of component units into a complete vehicle. (Most of these component units are themselves manufactured units which have already involved much work. e.g. engine, gear box, axle assemblies, body shell.) On the assembly line each employee performs repetitively, one small operation in the sequence needed to complete the assembly; and the unsatisfying nature of this type of job leads occasionally to lapses of quality and frequently to poor industrial relations. The alternative method is group production, in which a small group of workers is given a kit of parts and proceeds to build a complete vehicle, sharing the work amongst themselves. This method of working also lends itself to self-inspection. An automobile which comes off an assembly line is inspected in the factory, should be further checked by the dealer who sells it, but is finally inspected and tested by the purchaser. It is not easy to detect faults in a completed complex assembly like the modern automobile and impossible to fix responsibility for them when the vehicle was one of many passing down the assembly line. In group production, by contrast, each worker can be responsible for inspecting his own work before it is obscured by further assembly and it is not difficult to record which group build each vehicle. Group production is favoured for production in moderate quantities and it is a question of balancing speed (and perhaps low cost) of production by assembly line against the better working conditions and reduction of inspection problems of group production.

Of course the method of the future is assembly by robot.

Index numbers Comparisons are often more convenient, or even more important, than actual figures; and so index numbers are often used in statistical publications. One takes the value of the quanitity under consideration at a particular date (the base date) and the ratio of the current value to the value at the base date, multiplied by 100, is the current value of the index. The familiar example is the retail price index (RPI) which at present has a base date of January 1974. When the RPI has looked like reaching an inconveniently high level its base data has been changed; the RPI has been set equal to 100 successively in January 1956, 1962, 1974 and if it had not been it would now stand at about 700.

For other indexes the average of a year, say 1975, is often used as base and indicated by reporting the index as '1975=100'. An example of the necessary use of an index number is for the volume of advertisements for situations vacant ('help wanted') in the USA, since the ratio of vacancies to advertisement is unknown and a *number* of advertisements would be meaningless — one can only draw comparisons between different years. Index numbers are also used in OECD statistics of labour costs in member countries, thus avoiding difficulties with both exchange rates and differences in standards of living between different countries.

Isotope The chemical properties of a substance depend on the arrangement of electrons outside the nucleus, but its potentiality for nuclear energy depends on the structure within the nucleus. Most chemical elements include more than one substance, having the same chemical properties but different nuclear structures. These substances are called isotopes of the element (from the Greek 'same place') meaning that because they have identical chemical properties they occupy the same place in the periodic table of the elements. But some have nuclei which are more easily split than others, yielding nuclear energy, and these are called fissile isotopes.

New Deal When Franklin Roosevelt was elected President of the USA in 1933 the country was suffering from the depression which followed the Wall Street crash of 1929; and he proposed new economic measures under the general title of 'New Deal'. A wide variety of measures was tried (including the well known one of 'paying farmers not to raise hogs') but a continuing feature was the encouragement of cities and states to undertake public works, while the Federal Government lent them money and also sponsored some schemes directly.

'Normal' or gaussian distribution When a characteristic is spread over a large number of items, like IQ spread over individual members of a population, one can usefully ask two questions:
  (i) what is its most probable value?
(ii) how does it vary in the spread over the population?
(Statisticians use the word 'population' for any collection of items, whether or not the items are people.) If there are equal numbers above and below the most probable value, as is the case with IQ, then this value is equal to the average which for IQ is called 100. Next one needs to know the spread, and the measure most used by statisticians is called the standard deviation which for IQ is found experimentally to have the value of 15 relative to an average value of 100. But one could have the same standard deviation with most individuals close to the average and a few far away or with a smooth variation of numbers as one departs from the average, so it is necessary to specify also the shape of the distribution. A gaussian distribution, which results if a large number of causes is acting independently, describes the spread of IQ. This distribution used to be called 'normal', short for 'normal law of errors', but statisticians now prefer to call it a 'gaussian' distribution, after the mathematician Gauss.

OECD After World War II the US set up the Marshall plan, designed to give US aid to Europe so as to restore the economy of European countries by the end of 1951; and as a requirement was the maximum economic co-operation between European nations, the Organisation for European Economic Co-operation (OEEC) was founded in 1948. The UK and West Germany joined this organisation of 16 nations in 1949 and Spain joined in 1959. In 1961 the membership was extended to include industrialised nations outside and the organisation was re-named 'Organisation for Economic Co-operation and Development' (OECD) with objects
  (i) to promote economic growth, employment and a rising standard of living in its member countries;
  (ii) to contribute to sound economic growth of developing countries (which are not members); and
(iii) to promote the expansion of world trade.
The present 24 members are: USA, Canada, Japan, Germany,

France, UK, Italy, Austria, Belgium, Finland, Greece, Denmark, Ireland, Iceland, Luxembourg, Netherlands, Norway, Portugal, Spain, Sweden, Switzerland, Turkey, Australia, New Zealand.

The most obvious activities of OECD are publication of economic statistics and reviews of economic prospects of member countries.

Spot market for oil Most oil is sold on long–term contracts between producers and refining or distributing companies. But small amounts of both crude oil and refined products are sold for cash and immediate delivery in the 'spot' market. Prices may be favourable but continuity of supply is not assured.

Telechiric By derivation this word means 'remote–handed. Professor Thring applied it to the idea that machines only should enter coal seams, such machines being remotely controlled by miners who would remain in the safety and comfort of a central control room. But recent research by the National Coal Board (of the UK) has been directed towards developing machines which can automatically follow a coal seam, without remote control.

Value added (or added value) This is, of course, the basis of value added tax (VAT). At each stage of the manufacture and distribution of an article one may subtract from the selling price the sum of everything which has been paid to other firms for it and for any materials added to it. The remainder is the added value, which must be equal to the wages of employees of the firm in question, plus interest on capital and profit. Dividing by the number of employees gives the added value per employee; and if there is to be any margin for the payment of inerest on capital (including shareholders' dividends, the average value added per employee must be greater than the average wage per employee. The division of added value between wages and interest is the traditional ground for argument between employees and employer. VAT is distinguished from a simple sales tax by the fact that each concern in the chain of manufacture and distribution can reclaim the tax already paid by previous links in the chain, i.e. the tax component of the prices which the concern has paid for its inputs.

INDEX